How to Beat

Worry

T0385250

Also in the series

How to Beat Agoraphobia
Pamela Myles-Hooton

How to Beat Fears and Phobias
Mark Papworth

How to Beat Insomnia and Sleep Problems
Kirstie Anderson

How to Beat Depression and Persistent Low Mood
Mark Papworth

How to Beat

Worry

*A Brief, Evidence-Based,
Self-Help Treatment*

Liz Kell

ROBINSON

ROBINSON

First published in Great Britain in 2025 by Robinson

1 3 5 7 9 10 8 6 4 2

A CIP catalogue record for this book
is available from the British Library.

ISBN: 978-1-47214-915-2

Typeset in Minion by Initial Typesetting Services, Edinburgh
Printed and bound in Great Britain by Clays Ltd, Elcograf S.p.A.

Papers used by Robinson are from well-managed forests
and other responsible sources.

Robinson
An imprint of
Little, Brown Book Group
Carmelite House
50 Victoria Embankment
London EC4Y 0DZ

The authorised representative
in the EEA is
Hachette Ireland,
8 Castlecourt Centre,
Dublin 15, D15 XTP3, Ireland
(email: info@hbgi.ie).

An Hachette UK Company
www.hachette.co.uk

www.littlebrown.co.uk

CONTENTS

Section 1: Getting going   1

Section 2: Understanding worry   37

Section 3: Worry management interventions   69

Section 4: The relapse prevention toolkit   131

Section 5: Recovery stories   153

Workbook   181

Further resources   213

Acknowledgements   217

Index   219

GETTING GOING

Well done for taking the first step!

I'm really pleased you've reached out and started reading this book! In doing so, you've taken a first important step on your journey to recovery. Often, in order to get better, we first have to reach a point where we are willing to invest time and energy in this task. Psychological treatments involve a focused approach and require dedicated time if we are to achieve the full benefits they can offer, even if it can initially seem difficult to make time for them in our busy lives. If you are experiencing worry, as we will see shortly, this can be especially challenging as the worry can often be overwhelming and feel like it consumes a lot of our time and energy. So, as you work through this book, I ask you to take a leap of faith and prioritise your best efforts for this treatment. What I can do in return is help to break this down into small, manageable steps to support you through the process. With this approach, we will together maximise the opportunity for you to be able to beat your worry through the use of a brief, evidence-based treatment. The interventions and approaches I will cover have been used by health professionals to help people manage their worry for over thirty years. This means they have been tried, tested and refined over and over again.

I would like to cover the 'groundwork' in this section of the book by introducing you to what we mean by worry. I will briefly tell you about myself and the type of therapy this book is founded upon. I will also cover some tips on how to get the most out of this book and then together we will set some goals linked to both your hopes and recovery. Let's start by thinking about:

- What we mean by worry and related disorders

- Different treatment options

- How this book will work

- Top tips before you start

What do we mean by worry and related disorders?

What do we mean by worry?

Worry is something that everybody does depending on the stresses they experience in their life. The sort of worry we are talking about in this book though is when the tendency to worry is persistent and excessive. While the content of the worry may still be the typical things that most people worry about, these worries tend to be disproportionate, present for most of the time, feel out of control and cover multiple areas of life, such as:

- Work

- Relationships

- Family

- Health

People who struggle with this type of worry may experience symptoms that are in keeping with a diagnosis of generalised anxiety disorder (GAD). I describe that next alongside other related clinical diagnoses and the help that is available.

Anxiety disorders

GAD is a clinical disorder. As well as including a focus upon worry, it includes symptoms of:

- Restlessness

- Fatigue

- Problems with concentration

- Muscle tension

- Irritability

- Sleep disturbance

A longer-term consequence of GAD can be a strongly held belief that you cannot manage difficulties. This can mean you avoid trying to tackle any other problems that occur.

If you are struggling with any of the physical symptoms described above, there may be other resources that could be useful for you. For example, if you are struggling with your sleep you may find it useful to work through *How to Beat Insomnia and Sleep Problems* in this series. There are also relaxation exercises which can be helpful in dealing with restlessness, irritability and muscle tension. These are detailed in the 'Further resources' section at the end of this book.

Worry is the primary feature of GAD. Here are some key questions that can help you determine whether or not you are experiencing this condition:

- Would you characterise yourself as a worrier?

- Do other people in your life describe you as a worrier?

- Have you always been a worrier?

• If you currently have a specific worry, if that worry were resolved, is there anything else you would be worrying about?

These questions can help you to understand whether you are someone who a) is experiencing stress, which tends to be a short-term reaction to a particular situation, or b) has a longer-term tendency to worry which is present regardless of specific situations. This book is designed to help people who have found themselves in either of these situations.

GAD is clinically defined as when someone is experiencing the following symptoms:

1. Excessive worry and anxiety related to a number of different events or activities, on the majority of days for at least six months.

2. Difficulty in controlling worry, including feeling as if something awful might happen.

3. At least three of the following:

   a. Feeling restless or 'on edge'

   b. Feeling easily tired or having little energy

   c. Finding it hard to concentrate or your mind 'going blank'

   d. Feeling irritable or easily annoyed

e.   Experiencing disturbed sleep

f.   Having tight or painful muscles

You can gauge the severity of these symptoms of GAD by completing the Generalised Anxiety Disorder Questionnaire 7, commonly known as the GAD-7, which consists of seven questions and is freely available on the internet. At the time of writing, you can access this through: https://patient.info/doctor/generalised-anxiety-disorder-assessment-gad-7.

There are a number of other anxiety-related disorders which can feature worry as a common symptom. These include health anxiety (also sometimes known as illness anxiety disorder) and social anxiety. In the case of health anxiety, the worries centre around the idea that you either have, or will get, a serious illness. This is often also associated with hyper-vigilance about your health and monitoring for signs of illness. This can also be a focus in GAD but the range of worry always extends into other areas as well. In the case of social anxiety this links to a persistent fear associated with personal performance and others' judgements while within social situations. Panic attacks are also a common anxiety-related problem. This is less directly linked to worry, but people can report experiencing worries about having panic attacks in the future. The box below explains what a panic attack is.

What is a panic attack?

A panic attack is a type of fear response. They can be understood as an exaggeration of your body's 'normal' reaction to danger, stress or excitement.

During a panic attack, strong physical symptoms can build up very quickly. While these are different for each person, they commonly include:

- Racing heartbeat

- Breathlessness or feeling like you're choking or can't breathe

- Feeling faint, dizzy or light-headed

- Feeling sick

- Feeling hot, sweaty, trembling or shaking

- Pain in your chest

- Feeling disconnected from your mind, body or surroundings

During a panic attack it is common to have thoughts such as:

- I'm going to faint

- I'm having a heart attack

- I'm going to die
- I'm losing control

If these are symptoms that you experience, there are some useful resources to help you in the 'Further resources' section towards the end of this book. It may also be useful to speak to your family doctor.

If any of these descriptions sounds like the focus of the worries that you are experiencing (rather than the wider scope of worry that is experienced with GAD), it would be worth having a conversation with your local doctor or health professional. They may be able to suggest an alternative psychological intervention for you. It is also common when people are struggling with their emotional wellbeing in some way to experience symptoms of low mood. There is a lot of evidence to show that many people can experience GAD and depression at the same time. If this is the case for you, you may also find it helpful to read *How to Beat Depression and Persistent Low Mood*. Generally speaking, when both worry and low mood are occurring, it is usual to focus on the low mood symptoms first as this can then help the worry to settle. However, where the worry is the cause of your low mood, or if it would get in the way of helping you improve your low mood, it is useful to first learn ways to manage the worry.

While these conditions cannot be diagnosed solely on the basis of the descriptions I have provided above, hopefully this information will be helpful in allowing you to determine whether you have any other ongoing difficulties which might benefit from additional support.

Before we move on, it would be useful to fill in the GAD-7. There is space on Worksheet 1 (page 185) for you to write today's date and your total score. I would encourage you to complete this once a week while you are working through this book. Worksheet 1 gives you space to keep a record of these scores so that you can track any changes. There is also a graph for you to plot your scores on to help monitor progress. If you are borrowing the book or wish to leave the book 'clean' (in case you think you might use it again or lend it to someone else), you can either photocopy the blank worksheets in the 'Workbook' section (page 181) or print them out from: https://overcoming.co.uk/715/resources-to-download.

This table shows you how to interpret your score:

Interpretation of GAD-7 scores	
Score range	Category of symptoms
0–4	none/minimal
5–9	mild
10–14	moderate
15–21	severe

Please remember that a health professional will never diagnose or make a decision based on this questionnaire alone. Generally speaking, a score of eight or above is an *indication* that you are experiencing symptoms of GAD at a level that would warrant treatment. However, even if you score below eight, if you are experiencing any of these symptoms you are still likely to benefit from the work we will do together. The GAD-7 is not a diagnosis tool, but can suggest that you are experiencing symptoms which *might* indicate you have GAD. Only a health professional can make a formal diagnosis.

I will suggest that you complete this questionnaire weekly once you are underway with the treatment. This will help you to recognise if it is helping, and also if there are any ongoing issues for which you may need to seek help from a health professional.

Suicidal thoughts and self-harm

Suicidal thoughts can be common for people who are struggling with their emotional wellbeing, particularly if they experience some elements of low mood as part of their difficulties. If these are something you're experiencing, it's important you know you are not alone! If you are troubled by these thoughts or have been beginning to plan how to end your life, please talk to someone about this as soon as possible. You can get support from your family doctor, and there are links to services that can support you in the 'Further resources' section. *Suicidal thoughts are not permanent.* As you start to feel better, these thoughts should reduce.

People struggling with their emotional wellbeing can also sometimes hurt themselves in different ways. This might be in the form of scratches, cuts or burns. This is a way some people cope with unmanageable feelings. They describe how it can be a way to quieten the thoughts in their head which they are finding difficult. These can include constant worrying thoughts. If this is something that you are doing at the moment or something you have been thinking about, I would encourage you to talk to someone about it, whether it's your family doctor or additional support options, such as those listed in the 'Further resources' section. At the time of writing, more detailed information related to self-harm can be accessed at:

https://www.mind.org.uk/information-support/
types-of-mental-health-problems/self-harm/help
ing-yourself-now/

or

https://web.ntw.nhs.uk/selfhelp/leaflets/Self%20
Harm.pdf.

*

Before we move on to how this book works, I'll first outline some other treatment options you may want to consider. In this section I'll also briefly tell you a bit about myself.

Different treatment options

Professional support

For some people, the appeal of self-help is using your own resources to solve your problems. This is a really good option. However, others may benefit from a form of support where a health professional acts as a kind of coach while they are using the self-help approach. In doing so the professional will be able to:

- Guide you in completing the tasks in this book

- Help you to identify and solve any problems that you may encounter along the way

- Answer any questions that you may have

Your family doctor may be able to see you more regularly over the time you work through this book, and in doing so, be able to act in this role for you. Alternatively, in many countries, it is now possible to receive support from a healthcare professional trained in motivating and guiding people working through self-help workbooks such as this one. These people are often called Psychological Wellbeing Practitioners (PWPs), Low Intensity Practitioners or Coaches. In England within the NHS these people are employed in Talking Therapies for Anxiety and Depression services (see the 'Further resources' section at the end of this book for details of how to access these services). In other countries, there may be a similar service and your family doctor should know how you can access this. Please remember that professional support should be available to you if you need it. Having someone to support you can, for some people, mean they are more likely to complete and get the most out of treatment.

Medication

Part of the appeal of a self-help approach (such as the one described in this book) is that you are learning to overcome your problems independently. You are not relying on other people or 'pills' for help. You are learning skills that make you stronger and will be there for you to use again if needed in the future. People can have concerns about taking medication. They are sometimes fearful that it might be addictive or cause unpleasant side effects. For people who are experiencing worry, the guidance is to consider medication only after you have first tried a psychological intervention like this one. It can still be useful to have a discussion with your family doctor so you can better understand all of the treatment options that are available to you. If you have any worries about medication, please also discuss these with your family doctor.

Cognitive behavioural therapy

This book is based on an evidence-based psychological therapy called cognitive behavioural therapy (or 'CBT' for short). CBT is the preferred psychological approach for GAD in 'NICE guidelines'. These guidelines are for health practitioners working in England and Wales and are drawn from the best research evidence.

CBT can be provided in a range of different formats. For example, it can be face-to-face (either in a room with a therapist, or via online software such as Zoom which has become more popular since the COVID pandemic) and also in a self-help format like in this book. I have already mentioned that you can generally get support while using self-help books from your doctor or another healthcare professional. The use of CBT self-help books as part of treatment is referred to as 'low intensity CBT'. It is called low intensity because, through this method, people generally require shorter and fewer sessions in their treatment than otherwise with the traditional ('high intensity') form of CBT.

Using self-help

One of the advantages of self-help is that you can use the tools described within the book at a pace that best suits you. Saying that, as with taking a course of medicine, the approach works best if you keep going with it consistently rather than trying it for a bit, having a rest for a couple of weeks and then picking it up again. Self-help is an empowering approach in that you will know that the benefit gained has been through your own learning and efforts. It will also help you to develop skills that you can use again in the future if you ever experience similar problems.

CBT is often mentioned in magazines, newspapers and in social media, so you may already be familiar with some of its principles. If this is your first experience of CBT self-help, flicking through this book may seem a bit daunting initially. This is understandable. You may worry about what lies ahead. Try not to do so. I have done my best to make this book as easy as possible to read and use and have followed what I know to be best practice in writing self-help books.

About myself

We're going to work together over the next few weeks and so it might be helpful if you know a little about me. Hopefully, this will help you to build a picture of me in your 'mind's eye'. I am a psychological professional with twenty years of experience helping people with very similar issues to you. For the most part, I have worked in a role similar to the ones I mentioned earlier, as a Psychological Wellbeing Practitioner (PWP). I worked alongside family doctors and other health professionals, supporting people to work through evidence-based self-help techniques. I met with them regularly to help understand their difficulties, to introduce them to different techniques and workbooks, as well as to review and help them understand the most useful aspects of their progress.

I have also worked as both a supervisor and manager of Psychological Wellbeing Practitioners. In doing so I supported their safe, effective work with clients. For the last ten years I have worked in a university, where I have led the training for Psychological Wellbeing Practitioners. I have been involved in the development of resources to support people to undertake this work and I have contributed to textbooks about the work of psychological practitioners. Outside my work, I enjoy spending time with my family and friends. I have always loved music, both playing in musical groups and listening to it live. I try to spend as much time as I can in the countryside, especially since becoming a dog owner!

How this book will work

There are elements of this treatment approach that may mean this book is somewhat different to others you have read. Below, I describe how you can make use of this book to allow you to make the best progress possible in overcoming your GAD.

Using this book

While the approach described in this book works best if you apply it consistently, this does not mean that you have to read the whole book in one go. In fact, quite the opposite! It is best to work through the book in stages. For each person who uses the book, these stages may take a different length of time. A ballpark figure, however, for the whole treatment, depending on how significant your worries are, will be that you will need to invest some time into the treatment – most days, for around six to twelve weeks. It is better to take things steadily and have repeated experience of success, rather than attempt to move on too quickly and risk having set-backs. The book sections should allow you to pace yourself, like a marathon runner breaking their training down into many different runs to make it more manageable.

It may be that a healthcare professional has recommended this self-help book to you and you are working through it together with them in a coaching role. If this is the case, they will be able to help you as needed with some of the exercises, much like a coach would help someone train for a marathon. You or they could write down in the 'Workbook' section some of the examples that you develop together during your meetings.

If you are embarking on this treatment on your own, as you go along you may wish to record particularly helpful points together with their page numbers in the 'Notes' section of the workbook. Some people find this really useful. If you are not sure about something, remember that another advantage of using a self-help book is that you can simply go back and read that section again. If you need to do this, please don't become frustrated or self-critical – remember that finding it hard to concentrate and becoming easily frustrated can be part of the problems you are seeking help with in the first place! Take your time. The most important thing from my perspective is that you eventually understand the techniques that are described within the book.

Case examples

I want to talk a little about the case examples which will be used in this book: Therese and Mandeep. These are fictitious characters compiled from the stories of many real patients. Their examples will help you to understand the nature of their worries and how they learned to manage them by using simple techniques in their day-to-day lives. I will introduce you to Therese and Mandeep in Section 2, and to techniques that helped them in Section 3.

Overview of the book

Some people like to read through the whole book first and then go back and start using the techniques. Others prefer to use the techniques straight away after reading a section. Whatever you find to be the most helpful is fine: the key thing is that when you are ready, put the techniques into practice in your daily life. You may need to prioritise this programme and reorder your schedule for a few weeks in order to allow this to happen. Alternatively, you might not be doing very much at the moment because of your difficulties and so this will not be necessary. Within this book are activities designed to prepare you for change. Try to complete these activities as you work through it.

I have broken the book down into five sections. You can move through the book in any way that you feel will be the most helpful for you. You may wish to start your treatment by hearing about how other people have used the approach to help them overcome their worries. This can give you a good overview of the treatment and may help boost your confidence before you commit to changes yourself. If so, turn to the two recovery stories in Section 5. Here, Therese and Mandeep describe what they did to beat their worries. When you have finished Section 5, you can turn back and work through the rest of the book. Alternatively, you may be more inclined to start by learning more about the techniques involved in the treatment. If so, I would suggest that you work through the book, in order, from start to finish.

Sections of the book

Section 1: Getting going

This section focuses on how worry is defined and how it is different from some other psychological diagnoses for the purpose of this book. It provides an opportunity to complete the GAD-7 questionnaire to better understand your own symptoms right now and also to allow you to monitor your progress over the course of the treatment. There is also an opportunity here to set some goals.

Section 2: Understanding worry

Here you will learn more about the nature of worry, including how it can be affected by a range of external factors. This could be in relation to your work situation, your living environment or your relationships. You will learn more about how worry is maintained including considering what is maintaining your worry specifically. You will also meet some people who have experienced problematic worry themselves.

Section 3: Worry management interventions

Using the tools in this section, you will begin to understand how you can use the intervention known as 'worry management'. There are a number of different tools and stages within this that I will support you to implement for yourself. In doing so you will learn how to beat worry. You will be guided to help carry out the different techniques and how to monitor your progress. I can also help you troubleshoot any difficulties you might encounter along the way.

Section 4: The relapse prevention toolkit

Once you are feeling better, we will look at ways to ensure you maintain the progress you have made. This will involve reviewing what you have learned and making a plan for the future.

Section 5: Recovery stories

Here you can catch up with the people you met in Section 2. They share their stories of having struggled with worry and describe what they did to help themselves. You can see how they put their plans into action and continued to beat their worry.

Workbook

This section contains all the worksheets you will need to help you learn the skills to manage your worry. This makes them easier for you to photocopy, or you can print them out from here: https://overcoming. co.uk/715/resources-to-download.

Further resources

Finally, I have included details of relevant support organisations at the end of the book.

Top tips before you get going

Before we move into the next section, I want to share with you some top tips about the use of self-help books. These come both from people who have benefitted from CBT self-help and from health professionals who support people in using CBT self-help.

Top tip 1: Give it your best shot

"I've always been a worrier and have tried lots of times to learn to stop it. Sometimes it did get a bit better, but then I'd just fall back into it whenever things got stressful.

> The workbook helped me to better under-
> stand how worry was affecting me, and that
> really helped me to understand how the
> strategies in the book worked."

It is unlikely this treatment will be completely
'plain sailing'. There will be some challenges
for you. The treatment requires that you
keep moving forward in a paced manner,
so it's important you give it your best shot.
Follow the instructions and continue to use
the strategies. Think of it a bit like following
an exercise programme. If you go to the gym
every day for a week but then stop again for a
month, you won't make as much progress as
if you went three times a week consistently
over a longer period of time. If things become
too difficult, turn to the troubleshooting
guide in Section 3 or read the case examples
in Section 5. Revisiting these sections may
help to keep you on track. If a healthcare professional is supporting you, they may also be
able to help with the troubleshooting. They
may also be able to check you are using the
interventions in the best way and offer you
encouragement.

Top tip 2: Put what you have learned into action

"Once I understood the differences in my worries, and how many of them were 'hypothetical' [you will learn about this form of worry in Section 2], it helped me to see how I could hopefully worry less. This seemed to motivate me more and more."

People only benefit from psychological treatments if they result in changes in their lives. A therapist or a self-help book can only offer guidance and tools – it is up to you to put them to use. Generally speaking, with approaches such as CBT, the more effort people put in, the greater the benefit they experience in return. So, putting these tools and techniques into action is the key to getting better. Think of it as a bit like learning a musical instrument: the teacher offers the teaching and instruction, but it is up to the student to practise. Without investing time in this, the student is unlikely to make any progress between lessons. The lessons alone won't make someone proficient. The upside is that once you've started to see positive results, your confidence in your own abilities will begin to grow, and you'll know that if you ever experience difficulties in the future, you'll have found a way to overcome them before.

Top tip 3: Writing in the book is allowed – in fact, it is encouraged!

> "As I improved, I kept looking back over my worksheets and notes. I could see how much progress I was making. It really helped motivate me to continue."

As part of this treatment, it is really import-ant that you remember the tools and tech-niques that are described in this book. The book also contains written exercises which will prepare you for your treatment and maintain your progress after it is finished. To help with this I really encourage you to write in this book (as I hope you did for your GAD-7 score earlier). The 'Workbook' section is included for this purpose. If you have borrowed this book, from a library for example, and wish to keep it clean, you can either photocopy the sections or down-load them from here: https://overcoming. co.uk/715/resources-to-download.

To make this easier for you, each time you are invited to do some writing, I have included this image. This is intended as a reminder for you to put pen to paper. As well as helping you in your treatment, writing things down can really boost your confidence by allowing you to look back later and see the progress you have made.

Top tip 4: Like everybody, expect to have both good and bad days

> **"I was really frustrated when I found myself worrying a lot again halfway through the treatment; I was really disappointed. I kept on going, though. I kept using the worksheets and things started to get better again. Looking back now I can see that there was a specific reason why that happened – it was more of a reaction to a change at work rather than me slipping backwards."**

Within your treatment, I do hope that things progress smoothly for you. For many people this is generally the case. However, it is not uncommon to have the odd set-back. I will encourage you to think about these as opportunities for problem-solving rather than experiences of failure. As you understand how you react and behave in the face of different worries and challenges, you will be able to fine-tune treatment to allow you to continue to make progress. I will also help you to do this in the troubleshooting section within Section 3.

Top tip 5: Include friends and family if you can

"I described the treatment I was using to my friend and they offered to help me with it. Over treatment we met for a coffee every couple of weeks and we looked at my worry diary together and worked out what kind of worries I had."

There are many ways that involving others in your treatment can be useful, providing of course they are supportive rather than impatient or critical. For example, just the process of letting others know that you have committed to undertake the treatment can make you more likely to carry it through. In telling others, you have made yourself more publicly accountable for your actions. This can help to put a little bit of gentle pressure on you to keep progressing!

Involving others can also increase the support you receive through their encouragement. Sharing this book with them may also be helpful. If they understand the tools and techniques that you are using, they may also be able to help with any troubleshooting you may need to do. Most importantly, sometimes others' input may be essential for you to be able to carry out some of the tasks that will be involved in your treatment (you will see how others helped Therese and Mandeep in Section 5). In such instances, it can also be useful to meet with them regularly to check in.

Top tip 6: Set time aside to use this book

"I set myself a regular time to use the workbooks to help me keep using them regularly."

I strongly encourage you to schedule time to help you work through the book and also to follow through with the treatment tasks. This may involve some planning and rearrangement for the few weeks that you are working through the treatment tasks.

Top tip 7: Compare your progress to how you have been recently rather than when you were at your very best

"Meg (my PWP) suggested I try to focus on things I had achieved at the end of each day, rather than problems I've had. This helped me realise that I was making progress."

When you are caught up in your worry, it can be hard to remember the progress you are making, and you can fall back into unhelpful behaviours and ways of thinking. You may be having a particularly difficult time at work and have noticed you are worrying about this more. It may be though that your extra worries are only focused on this specific problem and you are not experiencing excessive worry in other areas of your life. It is important to notice this, as it can be a sign that you are only experiencing the type of worry that everyone naturally experiences at times. Try to treat yourself compassionately and stick to comparing your feelings in your current situation to how you were feeling last week or at the start of the treatment, rather than the very best you've been. This may be difficult initially, but it will become easier with practice and will help you focus on the progress you are making. Regularly reviewing your past GAD-7 scores and the records you complete in this book can help you with this.

Getting and using support

At times you might have thoughts about giving up the treatment. This is perfectly normal and to be expected. This might be because it seems too hard or you are starting to improve and so have less motivation to continue with the treatment. While both of these tendencies are normal, I would encourage you to try to keep going and complete the treatment.

This is the best way to help you to get better, stay better and maintain the progress you have made. I will talk about this more in Section 4. If you do get stuck and it feels too hard, try to remember the top tips I've just outlined. Who do you have around you who can offer some support and encouragement? It might be a friend or family member, or it might be your doctor. There are additional support options in the 'Further resources' section of this book. The troubleshooting guide in Section 3 also contains advice to help keep you on track.

It is also important to try not to achieve too much too quickly – remember the tale of the tortoise and the hare! If you keep moving, one step at a time, you will eventually reach your destination. Small steps help to keep you moving whereas setting off too quickly can risk you running out of energy.

Making change happen

Many people who would otherwise struggle to get started with their treatment have found the following activity helpful in starting to feel motivated. Consider the questions below and write your responses in Worksheet 2 (page 187) to help you focus on the change you want to make. You can write as much or as little as you like. Then I will help you set the goals for you to work on for your treatment.

How important is it for me to change?

Write down all the ways in which your worry is limiting your life. In addition, write down how your worry may impact on your life in the future if it remains the same or gets worse. How does/will it interfere with your ability to achieve goals you set for yourself when you are feeling well? What have you had to sacrifice because of your worry? Imagine that you go to sleep tonight and wake up tomorrow with everything in your life how you want it to be. In this scenario, worry is no longer a problem for you. Write down what your life would look like if this happened. What would be different? What would other people notice?

Do I have the opportunity to change?

I want you to imagine that this treatment will take, say, around an hour a day for eight weeks. To be able to prioritise your treatment for these eight weeks, what needs to change in your life? Do you need to change anything to support this (for instance buy a diary, a notebook, or learn how to use a smartphone app that serves these functions)? Is there some extra support you could enlist temporarily? Perhaps changing some habits could be helpful (for example reading this book every time you make yourself a hot drink, or having it to hand on your bedside table). Are there some things you may need to stop doing to give you some space to read about and carry out the treatment? Could some of the commitments you undertake for other people be reduced just while you prioritise your own needs for this programme? Write down what you can put in place to give yourself the best chance of completing the treatment.

Thinking ahead

In the last exercise, I asked you to consider what life would look like if it was no longer affected by worry. Now I would like you to think a little about the process of achieving this and getting back the life that you want. The way to do this is to break things down into more manageable and focused goals that you would like to achieve over the length of the treatment and beyond. Let's consider how your goals should be best structured. Try to make your goals:

Specific

For example, rather than setting a goal to 'not worry', think about what in particular is happening currently as a result of your worry. Think about what you want to be different or achieve in the future. Examples that are specific could be 'leaving work on time rather than staying late through repeatedly checking work' or 'enjoying reading a book on a Saturday morning'.

Capable of being measured so you can record progress

'Not worrying' is quite difficult to measure – remember, everybody worries some of the time! One measure of your progress will be a reduction in your GAD-7 score, but you can also be specific, for example by recording what time you finish work each day or how far you have got with a book that you were previously struggling to focus on because your worries were distracting you. Remember, everyone has good days and bad days, so it's important to view your progress over the long- rather than the short-term. Measuring your progress over the full course of the treatment can help with this.

Realistic for you to achieve

You might be inclined to set a goal of 'never worrying' or 'always being rational in making decisions'. While you might get closer to these things over treatment, they are less likely to be achieved completely in the time we are working together. Because everyone worries sometimes, 'never worrying' is unlikely to be a realistic goal for anyone! It is better to set goals you can achieve in the shorter term. This will then fuel motivation. You can revisit goals and make them more ambitious later in the treatment if this is needed. A more realistic goal might be to be successfully using a system or tool to support you with decision-making, or to feel able to focus on the things that are a priority (rather than your worry).

Framed positively rather than negatively

It is usually helpful to frame goals in terms of what you would like to gain or achieve rather than the things you want to stop. For example, a goal associated with what you can do more of will work better than just 'worrying less'.

When you have decided on the goals that are involved in your recovery, use Worksheet 3 (page 188) to rate each one in terms of the extent to which you are achieving this goal now. You can come back and re-rate them in one, two and three months' time to measure your progress. Set some calendar reminders in whichever form works for you (paper calendar or smartphone) to remind you to do this. There is space in the worksheet for three goals, but feel free to set yourself more or fewer if this is helpful.

*

You have now considered what your life would be like if you were to make changes. You have also set some relevant goals for therapy. Earlier, you began to make some plans regarding how you are going to schedule the time to begin your treatment. I hope that you now feel motivated and prepared to start soon. In Section 2 I am going to help you understand more about worry. This will lead us into talking about how to beat it in Section 3.

UNDERSTANDING WORRY

People who experience worry often have thoughts such as:

These thoughts often happen alongside their worries, which often start with 'what if . . .?'

In this section I will look at key information about worry and help you to understand the answers to these questions. I will then help you pinpoint in more detail how worry affects you and your life.

Features of worry and the connections between them

People usually seek psychological help for their worry because they are experiencing:

- Persistent worrying *thoughts* they feel unable to stop

- Areas of their life and their *behaviour* being affected by the worry (for instance their relationships, leisure activities or work)

- *Physical* symptoms such as poor sleep or frequent headaches

- Problematic *feelings* (for example, often people who are troubled with persistent worry can describe feelings of anxiousness or even sadness as a result of the persistent worry)

- A belief that their worry will result in harm (for example, that it will cause them to have a mental breakdown)

Cognitive behavioural therapy (CBT) assumes all these areas are connected and affect each other. For example, worrying *thoughts*, such as worrying about how well you are doing your job, can lead to *behaviours* such as working longer hours to check and re-check work, which can result in *physical* changes such as poor sleep and headaches. This can then have an impact on how you *feel,* perhaps caus-ing you to feel inadequate or anxious. Sometimes it can be helpful to distinguish between the content of worry – *your thoughts* – and the act of worrying – *our behaviour.* While usually behaviour is observ-able, in CBT we classify worry as a behaviour as well because it can be seen as an action or habit – just like other forms of behaviour. Our understanding of our worry can be helped by having some awareness of these connections. The theory behind CBT is that *if we are able to influence one area for the better through treatment, it is likely to have a positive effect on all the other areas.* You can see this in the 'four areas' diagram below.

While among people who experience problematic worry we will see similarities in how these areas are affected, everyone's personal experiences will be unique to them. Remember, everybody worries at various times in their lives, for example if they are struggling with money, struggling to complete a course of studies or have a big event to organise. We're not trying to eliminate normal feelings of worry – we don't want to turn you into a robot! Everyone is likely to experience worries from time to time. When worry becomes problematic though, which happens for some people, it significantly impacts various areas of your life and can feel persistent or out of control.

The function of worry

Stories of people with persistent worry

Now I will introduce you to Therese and Mandeep, who both experienced problems with persistent worry. We will hear more about their stories later in this section, and also in sections 4 and 5 where we will hear more about how they have used the treatment in this book. Many people find reading the stories of other people who have experienced worry and found ways to recover from it useful and encouraging. Hopefully over the course of this book they will give you some insight into:

- Different aspects of worry and the connections between them

- The challenges faced by people who struggle with worry

- What they did to recover

Therese's story

Therese is forty-two years old and works in a school office. She lives with her two children, aged twelve and fourteen. She split up with her partner, Sam, three years ago. She would describe herself as always having been a bit of a worrier. Over the last twelve months Therese has noticed that she is worrying a lot more and is starting to feel like she can't control her worry (*behavioural changes*). She has often been staying at work longer than her usual hours (*behavioural changes*) because she is really worried about making a mistake or missing something (*changes in thought patterns – the content of her worry*). She is also worried about what her colleagues think of her and whether she is doing a good enough job (more *thought changes*). Since Sam left, things are more difficult financially, so she is also worried about what would happen if she lost her job and, if so, whether she would be able to keep her house (*thought changes*). She is also worried about the impact this could have on her children. Her ex-partner Sam does still help out financially, but Sam has recently started a new relationship so Therese is also worried (*thought changes*) about how this might change things for both her and her children. She is not sleeping well (*physical changes*) and this is because she has all these worries going around and around in her head when it is quiet and she is trying to get to sleep at night (*behavioural changes*).

Therese's children are starting to notice differences in her *behaviour*. She is reluctant to let them walk to their friends' house on the next street, even though they were allowed to do this previously. She now insists on walking them herself as she worries that something might happen while they are away from her; for example, she worries they might be attacked or abducted (*thought changes*), so if she hasn't got time to walk with them then the friends have to come to their house instead (*behavioural changes*).

Therese has three close friends from school who still live nearby. She has always seen them at least once a month but recently she has sometimes not been meeting up with them (*behavioural changes*) because this will cost money that Therese is worried about spending (*thought changes*), especially on herself rather than her children. Therese has also missed seeing her friends on a couple of occasions because she has lost track of time with work she has brought home that she wasn't happy with when she left the office (*behavioural changes*).

Therese discussed this issue with her mother. She has always been close to her mother and she helps out with the kids sometimes. Therese's worry became problematic when she was taking exams at school and she received support from the school nurse at the time. Once she left school she seemed to 'get better' and the worrying just helped her to be organised and do things properly. Therese describes her worry as helpful to reduce uncertainty: if she can anticipate all the possible worst-case scenarios then she can be prepared for how she will manage them if they do happen. Her friends have also tried to talk to Therese about what is going on. One of them called her last week and Therese was able to talk to her about how she had been *feeling* anxious recently. Her friend said that her sister-in-law had experienced something similar and has sent her a book called *How to Beat Worry* which she had found to be really helpful.

Therese wasn't really sure how much a book could help her, but her children noticed it on her bedside table and also encouraged her to try it. After she started to read it, she realised that CBT self-help was something that had an evidence base for helping people who worry too much. It used a technique called 'worry management' (you will learn more about this in Section 3). She decided to give it a go. She also thought that it would be more manageable for her to do as she wouldn't need to find time to attend therapist appointments, and her mum said she would help if she could.

You can find out how Therese got on with the book in Section 5.

Mandeep's story

Mandeep is nineteen years old and attends university to study chemical engineering. He has always been very close to his family and has six siblings. He is the eldest child and was the first to leave home. His university is a five-hour train journey from his family home. He lives in university halls, has made some friends but misses his family. He is finding his course challenging and worries a lot (*thought changes*) about whether he will be able to cope with all the work, and how he will manage with the different work placements he has to do as part of his degree. He worries he is not clever enough to successfully complete all the assignments or that he 'won't be up to the job' in his placements. These placements might even include having to go and live in another country which he is really worried about (*thought changes*) as then he would be even further away from his family. It would be hard for him to support them abroad and he would miss them a lot.

Mandeep has got exams coming up soon and is staying up late trying to make sure he is prepared for these (*behavioural changes*). He is often tired during the day as a result and has occasionally almost fallen asleep in lectures (*physical changes*). Although he is spending a lot of time trying to study for his exams and coursework, he is finding it increasingly difficult to concentrate and focus on what he is doing (*physical changes*). He is really worried his tutors might have noticed this and formed a bad impression of him (*thought changes*). A lot of his friends on the course are going out in the evening, but Mandeep doesn't drink alcohol so he doesn't go with them very often. As a result, he isn't spending as much time with them as he used to with his friends at home (*behavioural changes*). He misses going to the cinema or just spending time at their houses and is worried his new friends might spend less time with him because he doesn't want to go to the pub (*thought changes*). When he has gone to the pub with them (drinking 'soft' drinks) he has found himself distracted worrying about what his family would think if they knew where he was (*thought changes*).

Mandeep has recently started cutting himself with an old razorblade (*behavioural changes*). These are only small superficial cuts on the tops of his thighs. They do not always even break the skin. They have never needed medical attention or even a plaster. He finds the physical sensation of the blade on his skin can help to distract him when the worries become too difficult for him to deal with: they force him to pay attention to the pain instead of his worries. He hasn't told anyone else he is doing this, and *feels* embarrassed about this *behaviour*.

Mandeep has always felt a huge family expectation to have a successful career, and also to get married and have his own family. As the eldest child he will be responsible for looking after his parents as they get older. He is worried about how he will get on with his degree in the future when he is already finding it so difficult (*thought changes*). He is also worried about the pressure to get married (*thought changes*). He has never had a relationship before and worries he would let a partner down if he wasn't able to provide for them (*thought changes*). He describes *feeling* inadequate and a disappointment.

Mandeep has recently disclosed his concerns to one of the tutors on his course. They took some time to talk about the course and placements in more detail and also recommended a book called *How to Beat Worry* that might be useful for him to look at. It was available from the university library. Mandeep was worried about how he would find the time to read this as well, but his tutor explained it is a CBT-based self-help book. It is written in a straightforward way and should enable him to put some strategies in place to make matters easier for him. It will guide him through the treatment step-by-step and he can also get some support from the university student wellbeing service to help him work through it. The CBT approach used in the book is called 'worry management' [we come to this in Section 3]. Mandeep thought it sounded perfect for his situation.

You will find out how Mandeep got on with 'worry management' in Section 5.

Questions and answers

Therese's and Mandeep's stories show how people have various problems with worry. You may still have some questions about the worry you are experiencing. I will hopefully answer these below.

Question 1: What are worries?

Worries are a type of thought. We all experience different worries at various points in our lives. Often we can separate these into two different categories: 'hypothetical worries' and 'practical worries'.

Hypothetical worries

Hypothetical worries are things we cannot do anything about and are usually related to the future. They often start with 'what if . . .' Everybody experiences these sometimes. Before going on holiday somebody might think 'what if I forget to pack something important?' A new parent might worry 'what if my baby never sleeps through the night?' When someone is experiencing problem worries, however, these thoughts do not tend to be just a single thought. They may start with a link to something practical or current, but they quickly progress into other thoughts that become less and less connected to the initial thought. Mandeep often experiences hypothetical worries and I've included an example here of the escalation that can happen with these hypothetical worries:

'What if I fail my end-of-year exams?'

'What if my tutors don't believe I can continue on the course?'

'What if they kick me off the course?'

'What will my family think if I don't have a degree?'

'How will I support my parents when they stop working?'

'Who will want to marry me if I have no job?'

'What if I'm alone forever?'

You can see from this example how the thoughts can become bigger and bigger in magnitude (with more at stake). In doing so they can become more and more detached from firm evidence when projecting into the future. Do you think these are worries that Mandeep could do anything about? Even the first worry is not a practical worry (see below) – although there may also be practical worries that he could address related to his exams (which we will consider later).

Practical worries

Practical worries are things that you can do something about. They are typically related to a current situation and so it is usually possible to come up with potential solutions for these. We know, however, that when people are struggling with persistent worries (which can often include many that are hypothetical in nature), this gets in the way of being able to concentrate and focus on coming up with solutions. In this way, people often have difficulty in sifting the 'wheat' (practical worries) from the 'chaff' (hypothetical worries). This in turn then becomes something more to worry about as well. The worry can feel so overwhelming that it becomes even more difficult to know which worry is the most helpful to focus upon. Throughout this book we will refer to these as practical worries.

Question 2: Why has my worry become such a problem?

Worry is something that everybody does and at times can be helpful, making us feel more prepared or in control. Worry like this is generally short-lived and can lead to helpful problem-solving. Long-lasting and frequent worry can generate more anxiety and further worry though. This can contribute to causing a vicious cycle of worry, which we will address in Question 3. Once this cycle is started, we can find ourselves worrying about lots of different things for much of the time. Rather than causing us to believe that we are more in control, we can perceive that we are spiralling out of control; that the worry is controlling our life. The worry can then start to feel like it is having a significant impact on different areas of our life.

Although the content of your worries may continue to be typical of the usual things people worry about, persistent worry tends to be disproportionate and present for most of the time, often without a specific trigger which prompts the worries. Some people hold positive beliefs (which you may not be consciously aware of) that worry is helpful. Examples of such beliefs are that worrying:

- Allows the person to always find solutions to problems

- Proves that they are a responsible person

- Prevents bad things from happening

Worrying can be understood as a misguided attempt to mentally solve problems. The worry is an attempt to reduce uncertainty by trying to anticipate all of the possible worst-case scenarios but instead can actually prevent positive thinking or effective problem-solving and action.

When a problem arises, people with GAD tend to engage in an endless number of 'what if . . .' questions. This is an attempt to prepare for all of the worst-case scenarios and predict all the possible outcomes. Unfortunately, each 'what if . . .' leads to another potential worst outcome, so as the process continues it becomes less and less related to the immediate problem that started the cascade of worries in the first place.

When trying to help manage worry, it is important to maintain a focus on worry as a process rather than getting caught up in trying to deal with the content of every worry. Perhaps you could think about it like trying to clear out a loft. Would it be more useful to spend lots of time trying to remember where different items have come from or what they are for, or instead put them into a box and take them to the tip or the charity shop? It will be putting things in the boxes that will allow you to clear out the loft successfully.

There are useful links to more information about generalised anxiety disorder (GAD) and worry in the 'Further resources' section at the end of this book.

Question 3: What causes worry?

Although there are lots of theories about what causes people to struggle with excessive worry, experts have not identified one specific cause. There are a number of different possibilities. These include one or several possible situations/experiences from the following:

- Stress or difficult life events

- A history of mental health difficulties in parents or grandparents (including problematic worry)

- Receiving direct or indirect messages from others, often important adults during child-hood, that worry is helpful in a world full of risks

- An imbalance of brain chemicals known as neurotransmitters

Day to day, worry can be triggered by a range of different things each time it occurs. This could be something obvious such as hearing or seeing upsetting information in the news, a particular personal stressful event occurring or being in a work situation you find stressful. Some triggers may be less obvious though. A thought or image might pop into your head out of the blue. Or a 'what if . . .' question might come into your mind for no apparent reason. This can be similar to unwanted or 'junk' emails appearing in an email inbox. *The response to that initial 'what if' question can affect whether the person either cascades into more worrying thoughts or is able to dismiss it and move on.* Moving the initial email into your junk folder may mean that you are less likely to get any more unwelcome mail whereas opening it is likely to increase the chances that more will follow. We will talk more about this in the next section.

The vicious cycle of worry

As mentioned above, when people are struggling with persistent worry, they have often fallen into what we describe as the vicious cycle of worry. The cycle is termed 'vicious' because the more people travel around it, the worse their symptoms become. I have drawn two examples of this below, based on

Therese's and Mandeep's stories. You will recognise this pattern from the model I introduced you to earlier.

Therese's vicious cycle of worry:

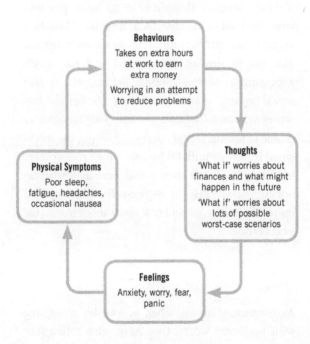

Behaviours
Takes on extra hours at work to earn extra money

Worrying in an attempt to reduce problems

Thoughts
'What if' worries about finances and what might happen in the future

'What if' worries about lots of possible worst-case scenarios

Physical Symptoms
Poor sleep, fatigue, headaches, occasional nausea

Feelings
Anxiety, worry, fear, panic

Mandeep's vicious cycle of worry:

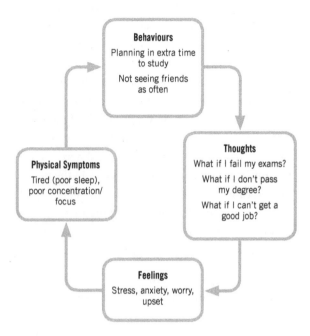

Question 4: Why me?

As I have already mentioned, there is rarely one clear specific cause for generalised or problematic worry, which means it can also be difficult to pinpoint a particular reason why you are troubled in this way. There is no simple explanation that can predict who will develop problematic worry and who will not. What *is* clear is that persistent worry is common. Worry was probably functional in our evolutionary past when our environment was more dangerous and unpredictable. At that point, when we were faced with threats such as wild animals or rival tribes, and did not have the safety of police forces and homes that could be locked at night, it made sense for humans to be more wary of possible threats. Worry can still be functional in certain modern situations, perhaps if you work in a dangerous job where there are different risks you might need to prepare for, such as in the police or the armed forces. However, for the majority of situations in our lives now, worry (and in particular hypothetical worry) is more like an unnecessary throwback to more primitive times.

Anxiety disorders are the most common form of mental health disorders. As we've discussed in Section 1, persistent worry can be a symptom of generalised anxiety disorder (GAD). What is important now is to work out what keeps it going for you and how you can begin to resolve it. This will help you both now and also in the future should you ever begin to experience similar problems again. Working through this book and putting its techniques into action should allow you to beat your worry.

Question 5: What can be done to stop worrying?

The good news is that there is a psychological treatment available that has been proven to effectively help people overcome their problems with worry. This has been extensively researched and is known to work for the majority of people who use it. The approach is based on the psychological therapy I mentioned earlier – cognitive behavioural therapy (CBT). This approach is structured and practical, which means it lends itself really well to a self-help format. This consists of using self-help materials which contain the same content and techniques you would cover if you were seeing a therapist. The approach can be used without any support from a trained health professional, but having support from someone while you work through it can also be really helpful for some people. Many people seek this support from their family doctor or practice nurse, or in England this might be through your local NHS Talking Therapies service with a PWP (more information about this role is given in Section 1). For people based in England, details on how to access your local NHS Talking Therapies service is included in the 'Further resources' section at the end of the book.

Question 6: Will my worry be a problem again?

I cannot promise that after working through this book you will never worry again. Remember, everyone worries sometimes! But the good news is that the tools and techniques you'll use as you work through this book won't just help you right now but will also be tools and techniques you can use in the future if you think your worry might be starting to become a problem again. The majority of people who access some form of help with their worry do not have a problem with it again, but even if it does re-occur, noticing the problem quickly and doing something about it sooner can significantly reduce how much of a problem it becomes for you. If you can spot your 'early warning signs' that your worry is becoming a problem again then you can use the techniques that have worked for you previously to prevent your early warning signs becoming a bigger problem. So dedicating time and energy into a treatment like this book can really help!

In Section 4 I will introduce you to a 'relapse prevention toolkit'. If you do begin to notice signs that your worry may be a problem again you can use this to head off a 'relapse'. I cannot guarantee you will never experience problematic worry in the future but I can help you to develop the skills to manage worry differently so it has much less negative impact on your life. These are lifelong skills to help you to manage your worries and keep them at a 'helpful' level.

How is your worry affecting you?

So far we have looked at how worry can affect you in four different areas:

- How it affects what we do (or do not do)

- How it affects our thoughts

- How it affects our physical feelings

- How it affects our emotions (feelings)

We have also talked about the different areas of our life which can be impacted when worry becomes a problem.

Now I would like to apply this understanding to your personal situation. To help with that, I have first provided an example of how worry affects Therese and Mandeep in four areas:

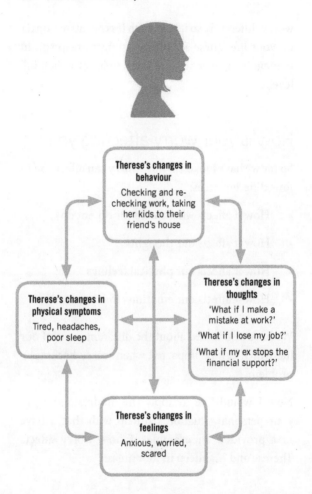

Therese's changes in behaviour

Checking and re-checking work, taking her kids to their friend's house

Therese's changes in thoughts

'What if I make a mistake at work?'

'What if I lose my job?'

'What if my ex stops the financial support?'

Therese's changes in physical symptoms

Tired, headaches, poor sleep

Therese's changes in feelings

Anxious, worried, scared

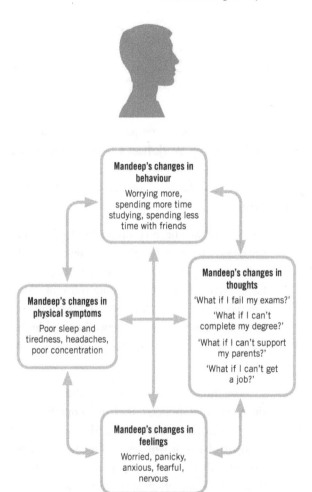

I would now like you to complete your own version of this diagram on Worksheet 4 in the 'Workbook' section (p. 191), which has space for you to list the symptoms and difficulties you experience linked to your worry:

1. For the 'behaviour' box, think about *what you are doing*. This may be things you have stopped doing or are avoiding. It may be things you have started doing or are doing more of. You can see from both Therese's and Mandeep's examples that there were things they had both started doing and things they had stopped or reduced.

2. In the 'thoughts' box, consider the kind of *thoughts (and images) that go through your mind* when you are worrying. These are likely to mainly be your worries, and many are likely to start with 'what if . . .', but there may be other thoughts as well which are useful to notice.

3. In the 'feelings' box, try to describe the *feelings or emotions* you notice. 'Worried' can describe

an emotion, but there may be others as well. 'Anxious' is a very common one. Typically emotions are just one word, like the ones that Mandeep and Therese have recognised.

4. In the 'physical symptoms' box, what *physical changes in your body* have you noticed or do you experience when you are worrying?

As we saw earlier, and as you can now see on your own diagram in worksheet 4, these four different categories can both interact with and fuel each other. Making changes in one area should stop or break the vicious cycle of worry we talked about earlier. The CBT model suggests that we can best do this by making changes in the behaviour and thought boxes. The treatment I am going to introduce you to in this book will help you make some changes in both. This will allow you, in a graded manner, to reduce how much time you are spending worrying, and also to reduce the power and impact of your worry on the different aspects of your life we identified earlier. This can then help turn the cycle into a new positive, or 'virtuous', cycle. A virtuous cycle is where we see a pattern of symptoms reducing and these improvements then fuel further improvements. This new virtuous cycle helps you beat your worry.

You can see Therese's virtuous cycle below:

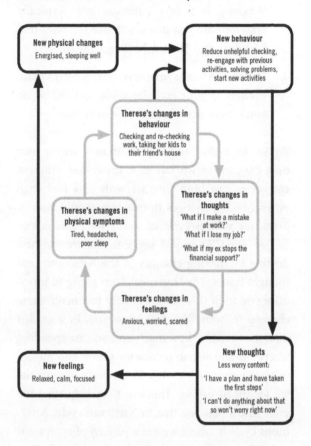

It probably took time for your vicious cycle of worry to develop, which means it will also take time to reverse it and turn it into a virtuous one. I am here to show you the steps you can take to allow this reversal to begin. The biggest step is acknowledging that you really want to change. You have already done that by starting with this book. You have also already thought about some goals or your treatment and how and when you are going to work on it. You are now ready to move to Section 3 where we will look together at how you can break this cycle and take the steps required to allow you to start to feel better.

WORRY MANAGEMENT INTERVENTIONS

If you have completed sections 1 and 2 – well done! I hope you've found the information about worry and the time to consider your own experience of worry useful. You should now have a better understanding of what worry is, what keeps it going and the wider impact this worry can have in different aspects of your life. Perhaps you can see aspects of your own worry in the theory and also in the examples shared by Therese and Mandeep? I'm pleased you've stayed with me so far and I hope you're reassured there is an evidence-based treatment for your worry.

If you've turned straight to this section, either because you want to get going with the intervention straight away or because you already have a good understanding of worry, then welcome aboard!

In terms of your own personal difficulties with worry, I hope you were able to helpfully compare them to the experiences of Therese and Mandeep. If you haven't yet completed the exercise on Worksheet 4 (in the 'Workbook' section) it would be useful to do this now. Please turn to pages 64 and 65 and use this information; the content of that exercise will be really helpful in this section. Some variation is natural, but if your symptoms have a different general pattern to those which I described in the earlier section, it may be that you have a problem other than worry. This could be one of the other anxiety problems we discussed in Section 1, or a problem that exists alongside your worry. If this is the case, if you have not done so already, it would be worthwhile talking to your family doctor before reading any further to confirm that this is the right treatment for you.

If you have not read or completed these parts of Section 2 already, please refer back to the vicious cycle of worry to remind yourself how worry is maintained (pages 55–7). The other important tasks for you to complete are:

- Your GAD-7 score (pages 9–10 and Worksheet 1)

- Your goals (pages 33–6 and Worksheet 3)

These activities will help you begin to work through this next section.

Now it's time to break into your vicious cycle of worry and start to enter a virtuous one. In this section, we're going to work together through an intervention called 'worry management'. This is an intervention that's part of cognitive behavioural therapy (which I introduced in Section 2). CBT contains many different interventions for different psychological problems, but research has shown that for the people for whom this book is designed, worry management is likely to be all they need to help them overcome their problems. Next, you will learn about worry management and how it works.

Points to remember

You are in charge of your treatment. If you are not clear about anything, feel free to re-read the relevant parts of this book again. If you have made notes either in the 'Workbook' section, a copy of it or in a separate note-book, these can be useful reminders. Feel free to keep going with this. It can be useful to keep a note of the things that stand out for you. The key thing is to use this book to *apply* worry management and put it into action to change your life. While reading the book without starting to take these actions may still be helpful, it will probably not be enough to overcome your problems with worry.

What is worry management?

Worry management is a scientifically established intervention which allows you to do exactly what it says on the tin – to manage your worries. *Remember, everybody worries.* Worries are a normal part of life. This intervention is helpful for people for whom worry has become problematic; it is having a negative impact on their life. Worry management is a structured approach that allows people to get back in control of worry and help them reduce the impact that worry is having on different aspects of their life. It consists of the following stages:

- Worry classification
- Problem-solving

And/or:

- Worry management

Stage one: Worry classification

The first stage of worry management is learning how to better understand the types of worry you are experiencing. Most people who experience problems with worry are able to recognise that the majority of their worries fall into one of the two different types I introduced in Section 2:

- Hypothetical worries

- Practical worries

Worksheet 5 in the 'Workbook' section of this book (page 192) is a worry diary. This allows you to begin to notice and record the worries you are experiencing, classifying them as either hypothetical (H) worries, or practical (P) worries (I talk more about this below). First, let us look at example worry diaries for Therese and Mandeep.

Therese's worry diary:

Situation	What is the worry?	How anxious am I feeling?	What type of worry am I having?	
What am I doing, where am I, who am I with and what is happening when the worry occurs?		Rate from 0 to 10 0 = not anxious 10 = most anxious ever felt	Hypothetical (H)	Practical (P)
Half an hour before the end of the working day, on my own in the school office	What if I can't finish all my tasks before the end of the working day?	8		P

		A	
	H	7	
	H	9	What if I take my work home then forget to bring it back in the morning?
	H	9	What if my manager gets cross with me for not finishing it?
	H	10	What if I lose my job?
	H	10	What if something happens to them on the walk?	At home, the kids want to go to their friend's house three streets away
	H	10	What if they get hit by a car?
			What if someone attacks them?

Mandeep's worry diary:

Situation What am I doing, where am I, who am I with and what is happening when the worry occurs?	What is the worry?	How anxious am I feeling? Rate from 0 to 10 0 = not anxious 10 = most anxious ever felt	What type of worry am I having?	
			Hypothetical (H)	Practical (P)
Revising for upcoming exams, alone in university accommodation late in the evening	What if I fail my exams?	9	H	
	What if I get kicked off the course?	9	H	

In the pub with some course friends, including two couples	What if my family think I'm a failure?	9	†
	What would my family think if they knew where I was?	7	†
	What if I'm not a good person?	7	†
	How will I ever meet someone I can marry?	8	†

I now want you to have a go at this for yourself using Worksheet 5 in the 'Workbook' section of this book. It is not always easy to make these distinctions and it does take practice. It would be useful to try this over the next week to take some time to understand the types of worries you are experiencing and really practise being able to categorise them correctly. This is important as the treatment will depend on the particular form of worry you are experiencing. If you are struggling to identify whether the worry is hypothetical or practical it can be useful to look back in your 'mind's eye' at the situation you were in when the worry occurred and ask yourself the following:

- What am I worrying about?

- Is this a current problem?

- In theory, could I do something about this now? Is there an action I can take?

Let us think about how these questions might work with some examples.

The worry is about a family member's birthday. It is their birthday in three weeks and you haven't bought a present yet. The family member has always been difficult to buy for and you are struggling to think of what to get this year, especially as you have lots of other things going on at the moment.

The present needs to be bought before their birthday in three weeks – and if it is ordered online that needs to include delivery time (*yes, it is current*).

You need to start working through options and make a decision about what present to order or buy (*yes, there is an action to take*).

This is a <u>practical</u> worry.

The worry is about the neighbours who are building a new decked area in their garden.

The neighbours have said the work in the garden will start next weekend (*yes, it is current*).

There is a concern that the decking will mean the neighbours are overlooking your garden but you haven't said anything to them about it yet (*yes, there is an action to take*).

This is a <u>practical</u> worry.

If you cannot answer yes to the second or third question, then it is likely that the worry is hypothetical. Sometimes, people may have hypothetical worries about things that *might* happen in the future, often 'what if' worries, but that may have a practical solution. Let's look at another example.

You are worried about bumping into an old work colleague you have fallen out with and don't want to speak to.

You do not *know* this is going to happen, but because they live in the same town it *could* happen at any time (*it could be current but not with a specific timescale*).

Is there a plan you can put in place to overcome this specific worry? If you have a plan for how you will manage the situation *if* it occurs in the future, then this can help you to stop worrying about the risk of it happening.

If you think you could put a plan in place then you should categorise this as <u>practical</u>. We will discuss this more as we talk about the next stage of worry management for practical worries.

Stage two: Worry time and problem-solving

The majority of people who have problems with their worry do experience both types of worry. Often through completing a worry diary, however, it is possible to recognise that one type of worry occurs more frequently than the other. There are two different strategies used for the different categories of worry:

- Problem-solving for practical worries

- Worry time for hypothetical worries

The following diagram can help you decide which approach you need to use for each type of worry. I will then introduce you to the two different approaches in more detail.

We will look at problem-solving here first. Even if the majority of your worries in your worry diary are hypothetical, it would still be useful to work through this next section to understand what the process is, even if you don't think you have many practical worries right now.

Problem-solving

Well done for identifying your practical worries! We now turn to a treatment for these.

Problem-solving is an approach which can be used to address any practical problems someone is experiencing. This is a particularly useful technique in addressing practical worries. Many worries have a practical solution, but if you are experiencing lots of different worries, together they can appear simply too difficult and overwhelming to solve. Alternatively you may find that there are so many different solutions to an issue it is difficult to determine where to start. A structured process of evaluating all of the possible solutions, then helping the individual to choose and implement the best of these, can help solve problems and resolve this form of worry. It is a bit like having a to-do list where you can tick things off as they are completed, allowing your mind to move its attention away from them.

There are seven separate stages to problem-solving. Worksheet 6 (page 194) in the 'Workbook' section can support you with this and we will work through each stage now. You do not have to work through all these different stages in one go. You may find that just doing the first two stages is enough initially, then you can move on to the different stages at another time. It is important to pace yourself and do this in your own time. Remember the four areas diagram we talked about earlier: by making changes in our behaviour, we will also positively affect the other areas – emotions, thoughts (in this case worry) and physical symptoms.

Stage 1: Identify the worry

The first step is to identify a worry you have been able to categorise in your worry diary as practical. It is your choice regarding which worry to choose, but I would encourage you to perhaps choose one which causes you less anxiety initially, unless there is a time pressure that means there is one that is important to prioritise (for example, related to an event that is going to happen sooner than those associated with your other worries). Some people find it helpful, if they have identified a number of practical worries, to first number them in the order they would like to tackle them. That way, once one has been addressed, when they are ready they will know which one to tackle next.

I now want you to write down the first practical worry you want to address at the top of Worksheet 6.

Sometimes when we write a worry down, we realise it might have more than one step to it so you might need to break it down into separate steps and tackle only one at a time. For instance, the initial worry might be about your pet dog needing a medical procedure. There might be a specific worry about managing the cost of the procedure, but additional worries about taking the dog to the vets, managing the aftercare (such as remembering to give medication) and a worry about how well the wound will heal. Please take time to think about if there is more than one step to your worry when you write it down.

We will now use one of Therese's practical worries to try out the different stages of problem-solving: 'What if I take work home and then forget to bring it back to the office in the morning?'

Stage 2: Identify solutions

Once the worry itself has been identified, the next step is to identify as many solutions as possible. At this stage, it is important to just list *all* the solutions you can think of rather than try to decide now if it is a 'good' or 'sensible' solution. Even if it seems ridiculous, just write it down on the list for now.

It isn't always easy to begin the process of coming up with solutions but there are different strategies you can use to do this.

- It can be helpful to think about what you might suggest to a friend who was having a similar problem. Often other people's problems can seem easier to solve than our own.

- It can also be helpful to think about the advice that a family member or friend, someone you really value the opinion of, might suggest.

• It may be a possibility that you could also ask a family member or friend to help you generate solutions (although it is important you still consider them all equally and do not assume other people have come up with better solutions. It is also important that you don't start to rely on help or reassurance from others as this can become unhelpful.)

Often you will have been very creative in coming up with lots of possible worst-case scenarios with your worry. We want to channel this same creativity to enable you to come up with a variety of possible practical solutions. Remember, it is also important not to start rejecting potential solutions too soon in this process.

Here are the potential solutions Therese came up with for her practical worry:

Worksheet 6: Problem-solving

Stage 1: Identify the worry

'What if I take work home and then forget to bring it back to work in the morning?'

Stage 2: Identify solutions

1. Do not take any work home

2. Take the work home but put it back into the car when I've finished doing it tonight

3. Leave a reminder on the back of the front door to take it back in for the morning

4. Set a reminder on my phone to take the work back in with me in the morning

5. Make sure to put the work back in my workbag and leave it by the front door

6. Leave the work on the kitchen table where I usually have my breakfast so I'll notice it in the morning

7. Take the work upstairs with me and leave it next to my bed so I'll notice it in the morning

8. Talk to my manager about my workload

Now I want you to take some time to generate all the possible solutions to the worry you have identified on Worksheet 6.

Stage 3: Assess the strengths and weaknesses of each potential solution

The next step is to identify the strengths and weaknesses of each of the potential solutions you have written down. There is a separate worksheet, Worksheet 7 (page 197), in the 'Workbook' section to help you do this. Working through each one in turn will help you come to a decision as to which is the best solution for you. There are a few things which can be useful to consider as you work through this task:

- Do you believe the solution is likely to work?

- Will you have an opportunity to try the solution out?

- Do you have everything you need to implement the solution?

- Could the solution cause more problems or have unintended consequences?

Let us first have a look at the strengths and weaknesses Therese managed to identify for each of her potential solutions:

Worksheet 7: Strengths and weaknesses

Solution 1: Do not take any work home

Strengths:	Weaknesses:
If I don't take it home then I definitely can't lose it	I then won't get my work finished by the morning
I shouldn't be taking work home anyway as my kids don't like it when I work late	I could get in trouble with my manager for being more behind with my work

Solution 2: Take the work home but put it back into the car when I've finished doing it tonight

Strengths:	Weaknesses:
If it is in the car then even if I forget to take	I could forget to put it into the car by the time

| it into the office initially then at least I can easily go and get it

It will allow me to get my work done | I've finished with it in the evening

If anything happened to the car overnight then I would be in trouble at work for losing important information |

Solution 3: Leave a reminder on the back of the front door to take it back in for the morning

Strengths:	Weaknesses:
It will allow me to get my work done It is hard to ignore a note on the door so should remind me to take it to work	Could be a risk that the reminder could fall off the door depending on what I stick it with One of the kids could move it not realising it is important

Solution 4: Set a reminder on my phone to take the work back in with me in the morning

Strengths:	Weaknesses:
I can do it straight away so it is definitely going to work	None unless something went wrong with my phone
It will allow me to get my work done	

Solution 5: Make sure to put the work back in my workbag and leave it by the front door

Strengths:	Weaknesses:
The work will definitely come back with me as I always take my bag to work	I could still forget to put the work into the bag when I finish it
	I don't like leaving my bag by the door just in case someone broke in

Solution 6: Leave the work on the kitchen table where I usually have my breakfast so I'll notice it in the morning

Strengths:

It will definitely help me to remember to take it to work with me

Weaknesses:

Small risk I could still get distracted in the morning but feels unlikely

Solution 7: Take the work upstairs with me and leave it next to my bed so I'll notice in the morning

Strengths:

It might help me to remember if I see it first thing in the morning

Weaknesses:

Sometimes mornings can be rushed so I could miss it

I might be tempted to keep working while I'm up and in bed if it is in my room

If the work is in the bedroom I might be kept awake thinking about it all night

> Solution 8: Talk to my manager about my workload
>
> | Strengths: | Weaknesses: |
> |---|---|
> | I might be able to find a better way of managing my work without having to bring things home with me

My manager would better understand how difficult I'm finding things | My manager could think that I'm not up to the job

If there isn't a change put in place it could make me feel worse |

Now I want you to have a go at working through all the strengths and weaknesses of each of the different solutions you identified in turn on Worksheet 7.

It can be useful to also label each of the solutions with a 'yes' or 'no' and to use 'maybe' for any solutions you want to think more about as you work through each one. It might also be useful to talk to a friend or family member as part of this process if you can, to get their thoughts and ideas.

Stage 4: Choosing a solution

The next step is to choose the solution you think is going to work best for you. You need to think carefully about whether you have got all the resources in place you need to carry it out. For example, it looks like Therese's best solution is to set a reminder on her phone – but that would only work if she had a mobile phone she could use for this purpose and she has a habit of reliably keeping it charged. There may be more than one solution that could work and if so, you may need to evaluate carefully regarding which one is likely to have the best outcome.

I now want you to write down your chosen solution in the Stage 4 box on Worksheet 6.

Stage 5: Planning the solution

It is important that you take the time to carefully plan how you are going to implement your solution.

You may need to break this down into a number of steps. It can also be helpful to consider the resources you might need, whether support from friends or family would be helpful, or whether there are any implications in terms of finances or equipment. Ensure that all the steps in your plan are specific, linked to the solution and realistic.

To help ensure the steps are specific, it can be useful to consider the following questions:

- What are you going to do?

- Where are you going to do it?

- When are you going to do it (try to set a specific time as well as day)?

- Who will you be with?

Let us now have a look at Therese's plan for her chosen solution.

Therese's plan:

Therese's chosen solution was to set a reminder on her phone to make sure she didn't forget to take her work back to school with her in the morning.

Step 1: She decided to set a reminder at the time she came up with the solution, as she did not want to risk forgetting to set it later.

Step 2: She decided she would set the alarm for ten minutes before the usual time that she left for work so she would have time to retrieve her papers from her desk at home without making herself late.

Step 3: She considered telling her children about the plan. As she would be with them at the time, they could also remind her. However, she decided not to tell them as she didn't want to risk involving them in her worry issue in case it created unnecessary worry for them. She also wanted to avoid seeking reassurance through this option as this was less likely to build confidence in her own ability to cope.

I now want you to write out your action plan for your chosen solution. It might be useful for you to first make some notes in the 'Notes' section of the workbook as you work through the questions I've suggested to help you get all the details you need for your plan. I then want you to write down the details of your planned solution, including its different steps, on the problem-solving worksheet (Worksheet 6).

Stage 6: Trying the solution

Now is the time for you to put your plan into action. It will be helpful for you to write down the detail of how you are to go about doing this and the steps that you need to follow as I have described in Stage 5. This way, if any part of the plan doesn't work you can look back at these details to determine what other options and solutions you have remaining (I'll talk about this more in Stage 7) and at what stage in the plan you encountered a problem. You may also want to consider using a calendar or phone reminder to support you in successfully implementing your plan.

Stage 7: Reviewing how it went

It is important that within this process you review how successful the solution has been and how you felt while you were doing it. It is helpful to do this as soon as possible after you have implemented your chosen solution.

Hopefully, the solution has worked well for you and you have been able to resolve the problem. Don't worry if this is not the case though. Problems can be hard to solve and can take more than one attempt. Part of the reason for generating so many solutions earlier in the process is so that you have other solutions to consider if the first didn't work as well as you'd hoped.

First, let's look at Therese's review.

Therese's review

"I identified a solution that I could carry out straight away, so the planning stage was quite short this time.

I was pleased I'd been able to come up with a simple solution and felt confident that it would work. I did check that my phone was definitely charging a couple of times before I went to bed. One of my concerns was that the reminder wouldn't go off.

The solution went really well for me this time. The reminder went off and I already had the work in my bag ready to go. I was really pleased I'd had the reminder though as well. I had also got my work finished that evening while my children were doing their homework. I still had some time with them later in the evening before they went to bed, so I did feel like it was the right solution this time.

I know I'm going to have to come up with other solutions as I can't keep relying on taking work home with me all the time. Now this has gone so well though, I feel more confident that I might be able to get on top of that as well."

On Worksheet 6 I now want you to make some notes on how your action plan went.

If the solution has worked, it is useful to think about what you have learned from implementing your plan. Here are some questions to help you think this through:

- What things helped make it a success?

- Did you have support from someone?

- Was it the option you thought would be best before evaluating strengths and weaknesses?

- Was there anything else that would have been useful to include in your action plan to make it easier or more successful?

If the solution has only partly worked and there is an aspect of a situation that remains an issue, there are a number of factors to consider:

- At what stage of the action plan did it stop working?

- Do you know what caused it to stop working?

- Would it be useful to work through the problem-solving process again for just the aspect that didn't work?

- If you look back at Stage 4, is there a different solution you could try that might work more effectively?

- Are there any other solutions you can now think of that might work better?

If you decide you want to try one of the different solutions, it is important that you return to Stage 4 and work through each section again. You might now be able to identify additional strengths and weaknesses in the different potential solutions.

If the solution hasn't worked, it is important to first consider why it was unsuccessful.

- Did something unexpected happen that interfered with the solution?

- Did some aspect of the action plan not allow you to carry it out as well as you'd hoped?

- Was there another weakness to the solution that you had not previously considered?

Once you have reviewed what happened and the reasons why it was unsuccessful, you can return to Stage 4 and review the other solutions you generated. Were there any other solutions you had marked as a 'yes' or a 'maybe' that you would like to put into action? It is important to start at Stage 4 and review the strengths and weaknesses again in case your learning from the first attempt has provided you with additional information that you can feed into your decision.

Working through this process can allow you to learn how to better tackle other practical worries. It has proven that you can come up with different solutions and that these can be helpful. It has also potentially generated solutions you might be able to use or adapt for other problems you come across. Once you have worked through the process a number of times, you will find that it becomes easier to create possible solutions for the problems that you've been able to identify and name. You will also start to find it easier to find the strengths and weaknesses of the different solutions the more you practise this.

Key points to remember:

- The problem-solving process can be effectively applied to practical worries

- Take time to work through all the steps

- Generate as many solutions as you can think of – even if they don't seem sensible

- There may be more than one solution that is a good solution for your identified worry

- Consider the practical resources and support you need to carry out a chosen solution

- It is okay if the chosen solution doesn't work or only partly works

- Review learning from the process – both for successful and unsuccessful solutions

- You can go through the process more than once for the same worry

I would encourage you to spend some time applying problem-solving to more of your practical worries over the next couple of weeks to really get used to applying the process. Hopefully, you will be able to successfully implement some really good solutions and address some practical worries.

Once you have worked through the problem-solving process a few times and have had the opportunity to understand how to apply this approach to practical worries you might be experiencing, you can then move on to look at the intervention to help address the hypothetical worries you are experiencing. Solving problems will have a beneficial impact on your worry: there is less to worry about if these problems are solved or you are confident you have a good plan to solve them. Continuing to record any new worry through continuing to use your worry diary will also help you to continue using this problem-solving approach for other new worries which may occur. Think about how best to use your worry diary: you might want to use a notebook to write things down, or use the notes function on your phone.

Worry time

Worry time is helpful, particularly for hypothetical worries you are experiencing. If you have chosen to use this book then it is likely you already know how difficult it is to stop focusing on your worries. People may have said to you 'just don't think about it'. Often, however, as soon as someone tells us not to think about something, it can make it seem like the biggest and strongest thought we have in our minds! If I ask you not to think about a pink elephant, what happens? For many people, a pink elephant pops into their mind's eye. The pink elephant might suddenly appear on this page, or become jumbled up with your other thoughts. I know *I'm* now thinking about pink elephants!

It is important to learn how to 'let go' of your hypothetical worries so you're able to spend less time focused on them. This is not always so straightforward to do. Worry time is a structured way of learning how to 'let go' of these worries, which will help to lessen the impact they are having on the different areas of your life.

Worry time allows you to have a structured amount of time at a regular interval where you can focus on your worries at a time that is convenient for you. This dedicated time allows you to let go of worry more easily at the time it occurs because you know you can focus on it later. As long as you have written the worry down, there is no risk it will be forgotten, which allows you to put it out of your mind until the worry time. This then means that the worry is less likely to be experienced at other times. Remember the four areas diagram: worry time enables you to make positive changes in the 'thoughts' box by changing the content of your thoughts. This in turn enables positive changes in the other three areas: behaviour, mood and physical symptoms.

Worry time has been shown to be really helpful for many people and can help put you back in control of your worries. It will help you to see that worries do not need to take over your life. Scheduling worry time can help you reduce the impact of your hypothetical worries on other aspects of your life.

We will now look at the different steps in worry time.

Step 1: Schedule your worry time

The first step is to decide when is going to be the best time for you to use worry time. Think about a time each day that you could set aside to worry about your hypothetical worries. People often find that around twenty minutes is a good amount of time for this, but it can vary between fifteen and thirty minutes. Start with what feels right for you. You can always change it slightly once you start using it.

It is important that the time you schedule can be protected for you to worry about your hypothetical worries, and you aren't going to be disturbed by work, children or other distractions. It is also really important that you do not plan your worry time to occur too close to your bedtime. If you decide that evening is the best time for this, make sure it is early enough that you can then do something else before going to bed.

Whatever time of day you choose to schedule your worry time for, it is useful to know what task you will be undertaking afterwards. Ideally this will be something mentally engrossing and not linked to your worry. If you schedule worry time for the evening, this might be watching a favourite programme or reading a book. If it is at an earlier time of day, make sure you have a specific task for after you have completed worry time. I would recommend that you set a schedule for your worry time a week at a time.

Top tips:

- Make sure you will not be disturbed

- Turn your phone off or ask someone else to answer it

- Identify somewhere quiet to do the exercise, with no distractions

---

Mandeep's worry time schedule:

"My worry time is every evening at 9 p.m. for thirty minutes. I don't go to bed until at least 11 p.m. and often it is quiet at 9 p.m. as most of my friends have gone to the pub."

I now want you to write your worry time schedule for your first week at the top of Worksheet 8 (page 201).

Step 2: Writing down your worries

Although you have now scheduled your worry time, this of course will not necessarily stop worries from popping into your head during the day. Now you have your worry time scheduled though, so rather than giving the worry all your attention, you can simply write it down knowing that you have your worry time scheduled for later that day to give it your full attention then.

You will still be taking these worries seriously – I'm not asking you to try not to think about them. But if you write them down, you can feel confident you have accurately recorded them and can then re-focus your attention, knowing you'll have time to worry about them later.

You can use Worksheet 8 in the 'Workbook' section to write your worries down. Alternatively you may prefer to keep a note of them using the notes function on your phone. Writing them down and putting them aside in this way will allow you to re-focus your attention on what you need to be doing at the time. Think of it as having a shopping list you can add things to as you remember them: once they are written down you no longer need to hold them in your head. If the same worry occurs more than once at different times during the day, you can use the tally column to just keep a record of the same worry.

This can help you recognise if there are particular worries you have more often than others.

We will look at different ways to help you re-focus your attention in Step 3.

Remember:

There may be practical worries which occur during the day alongside hypothetical worries. It is best to just write down all your worries at this stage (we have already talked about taking time to be clear if a worry is practical or hypothetical). Once they are written down you can work through all of your worries on the list in worry time and identify which ones are practical. You can then take time to apply the problem-solving strategy we covered above at a time that works for you. You should not be working on practical worries with problem-solving during worry time.

There is an exception to this. If you have a practical worry that is urgent, you may need to come up with a plan to deal with it straight away. It is then important to prioritise tackling that particular issue. It will still be useful to use the problem-solving approach I have introduced above if there are different possible ways to solve this problem, but you may need to stop what you are doing in order to undertake the problem-solving depending on the level of urgency.

We will now look at Mandeep's list of worries he recorded for worry time.

Mandeep's list of worries

Worry	Anxiety rating	Tally
What if I fail my exams?	9	III
What if my tutors don't think I can do the course?	9	I
What if I can't keep up with the work when I'm on placement?	8	II
What if the people on my placement don't think I'm good enough?	7	I

What will my family think if I don't pass my degree course?	9	IIII
How would I ever decide what else I could do with my life?	8	II
How will I support my parents when they retire if I don't have a career?	9	I
Are my friends going to stop talking to me if I never go out with them?	9	I
How am I ever going to meet a girl if I'm just always studying?	9	II
What if no one wants to marry me?	9	I

You can use Worksheet 8 to record your worries. It is important to remember this is for you to use throughout the day rather than trying to record them all in one go by trying to remember them.

Step 3: Re-focus your attention

Once you have written your worries down, it is important you re-focus your attention to what you were doing just prior to the worry coming into your head. This may have been a task at work, it may have been something fun you were doing with your family or something practical you were doing in the house. It is not always easy to do this but if the worry comes back into your head, remind yourself that you have already written it down so it is okay to stop thinking about it for now. You can also mark it again on the worry list using the tally column. You are not ignoring it or trying to dismiss it permanently – you are just postponing thinking about it until your worry time. There you can give it your full attention without it having a negative impact on other important things in your life.

Tips for re-focusing

Really pay attention to the thing you are doing, even if it's a routine task like housework.

Each time your mind starts to wander back to your worries, anchor your attention back to the task you were doing. Think about:

<u>Touch:</u> What does the activity feel like (for example, are you typing, writing, ironing, cleaning)? Is it a rough or smooth texture in your hand? Where on your body are you in contact with something?

<u>Sight:</u> What do you notice about what you are doing? Does anything catch your eye? What is the light like? Are there shadows? What colours can you see?

<u>Hearing:</u> What sounds do you notice? Are there specific noises you're making in the task you're doing (for example, the sound of typing on a keyboard or the sound of a Hoover)?

<u>Smell:</u> What smells do you notice? Do they change at all as you are carrying out the task? Are they pleasant smells?

<u>Taste:</u> What flavours do you notice? Are there any particular tastes at different times in the task?

You don't need to write down the answers to these questions but starting to ask yourself some of them can be really helpful to re-focus your attention back to your task.

I would ask you here to take a break from this book and have a go at using this re-focusing technique. It is helpful to have tried it more than once before you start trying to use it specifically to re-focus your attention from your worries.

As they continue to practise worry time some people notice that they gradually find it easier to re-focus their attention once they have written the worries down. This process is called worry postponement – you are learning how to postpone your worry to a different time of the day so that you can continue with whatever task you are working on at the time the worry comes into your head. This can then prevent the worries beginning to spiral as you re-focus your attention after only one or two worries have been written down.

Step 4: Using worry time

When you get to the time you have scheduled as worry time, return to your list of worries. These might be written on Worksheet 8 from the 'Workbook' section of this book or you may have them written down in the notes function on your phone. If you have used your phone to record them, think about how you can set up your phone so you will not be distracted by notifications, messages or calls. You might want to put it on airplane mode for the duration of your worry time so you will not be disturbed.

When you review the list, you may identify practical worries which you can use problem-solving to address. (Remember, you should not be using your worry time for problem-solving though. That can wait until after the worry time, or use another time that is convenient for you.) I would recommend you circle any practical worries you come across or write them down somewhere else. That way you have a record of them for when you want to try problem-solving with them. Once you have identified which are the hypothetical worries, you can then worry about them!

Take each worry you have written down in turn and make sure to properly read the words and consider the worry. Sometimes when you come back to your worries during worry time, you will find they are no longer a worry for you. They may have resolved themselves. They may just seem less important now you are reviewing them and not something you think you need to worry about. If this is the case you can put a line through the worry. If you realise a worry might have a practical solution, again, you can use the problem-solving process (Worksheet 6) to work through that process at another time.

Using worry time takes time and practice. Some people find it a bit odd initially to allow themselves to focus on their worries but remember: research shows that it is useful in reducing the impact of hypothetical worries on a day-to-day basis. Often people find that as they get into a routine of using worry time, they can begin to reduce the length of this each day. I recommend you don't reduce it to less than fifteen minutes though, to ensure you are giving yourself enough time to focus on your worries.

At the end of your scheduled worry time, it is important to take some time to review anything that you have learned from this. You can use Worksheet 9 (page 203) to record this review. Some things you might want to think about include:

- Did some of your hypothetical worries have a practical solution?

- Did you have as many worries as you expected to? More, or not as many?

- Was the focus of many of the worries related to the same thing?

- Did some of the worries not bother you anymore or not worry you as much as they did earlier in the day?

- Did you decide to end your worry time early?

As you practise the worry time regularly, you will start to get used to the process and hopefully it will feel less odd. Reviewing how the worry time has been each time is really helpful as you will begin to notice how it is helping you manage your worries and allow you to feel more in control of them.

Let us now look at Mandeep's review of his worry time:

"I was a bit apprehensive about how using the worry time would go. Through writing my worries down and categorising them, I realised that most of my worries were hypothetical. The length of the list was a bit overwhelming. I put my phone into airplane mode and really tried to focus on the worries. Some of them still felt really big, but there were a couple that I realised weren't really bothering me now and I felt able to cross out almost immediately. Focusing on them also made me more certain that they really were hypothetical and so I couldn't do anything to solve them. I found this really useful to notice.

I had given myself thirty minutes but after about twenty minutes I realised I didn't want to focus on my worries anymore. So, I decided to stop a bit sooner, knowing I was going to do it again the next day, which felt like a good thing. I felt a bit frustrated that there were still so many really big worries on the list at the end of the time, but then I knew it wouldn't all be better after one go, and some of them did feel less upsetting than they had done, even if I couldn't actually cross them out. I definitely know I will do it again tomorrow and carry over the ones on my list to the next worry time."

There is no set timescale for how long you should use worry time. Everyone will have their own experience of how long they find it useful. Most people find that after a few weeks they can begin to reduce the length of time they schedule worry time. This means that in practice there can be a natural, gradual process to stopping its use. Some people also choose to reduce its frequency and start doing it every other day before deciding when they might stop doing it altogether. Others continue to use it once or twice a week for a longer period of time. Either approach is perfectly fine so long as you find it helpful. It is helpful to also notice if there is any change in your weekly GAD-7 score over the period that you are using worry time. Improvement here can be a useful indication that it is helping.

Most people find that they notice a reduction in how many hypothetical worries they are experiencing after applying worry time. They also notice that any worries that remain have less impact on their life as they are able to postpone them and contain them within worry time. As a result, they feel back in control of their worries. As you continue to use both worry time and problem-solving this is how you are likely to feel as well. If you are not noticing any improvements in the amount of worry you are experiencing or any improvement in the impact that worry is having on you, I would recommend you go and speak with your family doctor. They will be able to determine whether or not you are able to make the best use of the interventions in this book. If this is not the case, another treatment approach might be better for your needs.

Below is the four areas diagram which shows where the two different aspects of worry management – worry time and problem-solving – impact on this cycle.

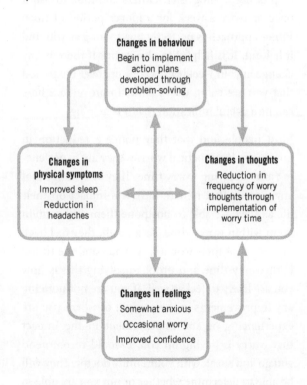

Changes in behaviour
Begin to implement action plans developed through problem-solving

Changes in physical symptoms
Improved sleep
Reduction in headaches

Changes in thoughts
Reduction in frequency of worry thoughts through implementation of worry time

Changes in feelings
Somewhat anxious
Occasional worry
Improved confidence

Troubleshooting

Hopefully, you're finding the strategies I've described here helpful and clear to use and are starting to notice a reduction in the amount of worry you're experiencing. I hope that you're also seeing a reduction in the negative impact this is having on the different aspects of your life you identified earlier in the book. However, if you've experienced difficulties with the interventions, here are some strategies that may help.

I am finding it hard to identify which worries are hypothetical and which are practical

Categorising worries can be really difficult at first, particularly if you identify some that could have a potential practical solution but are not an issue currently. For instance, you might be worrying about a party you have to go to in three months. If that is the case, you might find it useful to use problem-solving to come up with a plan regarding how you will tackle this once those three months have passed. Alternatively, you might decide that you don't need to worry about it yet and decide it is okay to leave it for now. You could then worry about it in worry time or use the problem-solving approach nearer the time when the content of the worry related to the event might have changed. What was previously a hypothetical worry might have now become a practical worry with possible solutions. Perhaps you could set a calendar reminder to include it in worry time or work through the problem-solving process in two months' time. This would allow you to let it go for the moment, but feel confident you can give it attention again as needed. This means currently you would categorise it as a hypothetical worry.

Categorising worries takes practice. The more you do it, the easier it will become. Remember to try to use the questions I told you about earlier: Is this a current problem? Can I do something about it now? It can also be helpful to ask, 'Is this *my* problem?' Can you do something about it or does someone else need to do something for it to change? If you have someone who is supporting you with this treatment, it might also be useful to discuss this with them. You can then try to classify your worries together.

If you classify a worry incorrectly initially, this isn't the end of the world – the other steps in the process should naturally allow you to re-classify it. If you have decided it is a hypothetical worry but in reality it is a practical one, during worry time it is likely you will identify something you can do about it. At this point you can reassign it as a practical worry for problem-solving. If you have decided it is a practical worry but it is in reality a hypothetical one, during the problem-solving process you are unlikely to be able to come up with concrete solutions that you can put into place. It is likely that in the first stage of this process, when you try to define the specific worry, you will notice if it is better classified as hypothetical. It is also highly likely you won't be able to identify any helpful solutions if the worry is hypothetical.

What is important is that you don't give up. The more practice you have in classifying your worries, the easier you will find it.

I find it difficult to come up with more than one or two solutions to practical problems

Remember that you are using the problem-solving strategy because there isn't an obvious solution to the problem. If there was, you probably would have found it already! Problems can be difficult to resolve, often more so when they're our own problems. It is important to take your time to work through the process and not be too hard on yourself when you find parts of it difficult.

Bring to mind the questions I listed earlier which can help in generating solutions:

- What solution would you suggest to a friend who was having the same problem?

- What do you think your friend or family member would come up with?

If you do have someone supporting you it can also be useful to try to come up with solutions together. However, I would encourage you to try to do so on your own first. It is easy to assume that someone else's suggestion is going to be better than our own. That isn't always the case. You need to consider all the solutions you write down equally during Stage 3, whether or not they are all yours. This will allow you to pick the best solution to your problem.

I'm really struggling to re-focus my attention once I've written the worries down for worry time

Re-focusing attention can be a really tricky thing to do. Remember that pink elephant, and how easily it can sneak back into our thoughts? It is okay if the worry comes back into your head: this is normal. Accept its return without getting upset. Then return to the re-focusing technique I introduced you to. Use your five senses to re-focus on the task again. Sometimes you might have to do this a few times before you are properly able to re-focus.

The more you practise this process, the more easily you will be able to re-focus your attention away from your worries and back to the task you need to focus on. If you find the re-focusing technique difficult to use, there are other strategies you can use to help. Some people find it helpful to sing (either in their head or out loud) or listen to a particular song. It is useful to plan ahead which song you will use to do this. Remember this process is about 'letting go' of the worry for now. So you could sing 'Let It Go' from *Frozen*, or you might prefer to sing 'Don't Worry, Be Happy' or 'Shake It Off' in a silly voice (whether in your head or out loud!). Alternatively, you just might want to use a favourite song. It can also be helpful to have a particular memory to focus your attention on, perhaps a favourite holiday or a special family day. Again it is useful to have a plan of what memory you are going to use ahead of time as then it will be easier to bring to mind if you need it. Keep in mind, *you have written the worry down so it is not going to be forgotten!*

I feel uncomfortable during worry time

A lot of people describe initially finding worry time a bit uncomfortable. This is understandable. You have probably been trying *not* to think about your worries for a long time. It is also very normal to feel uncomfortable when you are doing something new. It is useful to remind yourself that, even if you do feel uncomfortable, the longest the feeling will last for is the period of time that you have scheduled for worry time.

It is important that you don't start trying to distract yourself during worry time. Give your attention to the list of worries you have written down. Take each one in turn and re-read the words carefully. Don't assume you still remember what the worry is from when you wrote it down but, rather, carefully read it while focused on what you have written on Worksheet 8. Take note of the tally column to think about how many times that particular worry came into your head during the day.

The process of being able to cross some worries off the list can also help you feel more comfortable and confident. You can see that your list of worries is reducing. This is not something you are going to do forever but doing it regularly for a period of time is an established technique to help people beat their worry.

I don't know when to stop using worry time

Sometimes, it can be hard to recognise how much progress you have made. It can be helpful to review your weekly GAD-7 scores to see if this illustrates a reduction in your symptoms as you apply the strategies I've shown you in this book. It is important not to stop using worry time too soon, especially if the reason you want to stop is because you feel uncomfortable doing it. A number of signs can be recognised as evidence you're ready to reduce or stop using worry time:

- Noticing a reduction in how many hypothetical worries you are experiencing each day

- Being able to reduce worry time to fifteen minutes for at least two weeks

- Reduced scores on the GAD-7

If you do stop and then find your hypothetical worries are still a problem, you can always start practising worry time again.

What if by stopping worrying I miss something bad that causes me a problem?

If you worry a lot, you may believe that the process of worrying about potential, future problems helps to generate possible solutions that could be used in the event that these problems arise ('forewarned is forearmed'). Worrying in this way is an effort to predict various future possibilities so no nasty surprises arise. If you have thought of every possible thing that could go wrong, then you are no longer left with the unbearable feeling of uncertainty. You may therefore engage in *worry behaviours* such as reassurance-seeking or over-preparing by making multiple plans for different potential future scenarios. You may also avoid some situations altogether. Once you believe you have done everything you can to cope with matters if one of the predicted worst-case scenarios does happen, you then experience a sense of relief because you have increased the level of predictability around an aspect of the future. This relief can then confirm your belief about the usefulness of these strategies. However, it is useful to question whether this is always the best approach:

- Does thinking about the problem actually allow you to generate effective solutions?

- Does worrying about bad things that may never happen sometimes make you feel anxious even if you might be somewhat prepared for dealing with them?

- Have things ever gone wrong even when you have worried about them in advance?

Without changing or dropping these approaches there is no opportunity to see what the outcome might be in the absence of worry and the use of other more productive strategies that this new approach may offer. This can limit your opportunities to have experiences that *disprove* your beliefs about worry. Changing this pattern is an important part of tackling worry.

THE RELAPSE PREVENTION TOOLKIT

This section is for those who have already read the previous sections and have successfully completed them using the worry management intervention (which consists of either problem-solving, worry management or a combination of the two). I hope you have now broken your vicious cycle of worry and are making good progress towards the goals you made at the start of this journey. Through your own hard work, you have successfully helped yourself to feel better and beat your worry. Now we need to keep an eye on this to ensure you don't slip back into the vicious cycle of problematic worry. This is the final stage of the treatment – staying well and dealing with any difficulties you may encounter in the future. To increase the chances of maintaining the progress you have made, I would encourage you to work through this section. If you train hard and get fit through following an exercise programme, it is still necessary to continue training to maintain your fitness. The same is the case with this psychological treatment.

It is common for people to worry that they may lose some of the progress they have made or that their worries may start to become problematic again in the future (this is called a 'relapse'). It is important to remember that everyone experiences worry sometimes. But after people have made improvements to beat their problematic worry, they can have questions such as:

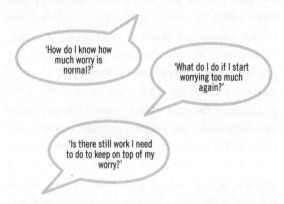

'How do I know how much worry is normal?'

'What do I do if I start worrying too much again?'

'Is there still work I need to do to keep on top of my worry?'

Once you are feeling better, understandably you want to maintain the positive changes you have achieved through your hard work. It can be frightening to think you might slip back and become limited by your worry again.

If a health professional has been supporting your efforts through the use of this book, ending your time with them can also produce concerns about whether you can now continue to cope on your own. It is important to remember that it wasn't the support from the professional that resulted in the progress you have made in overcoming your problematic worry – it was *your* application of the knowledge and techniques that *you* have learned in this book that produced your achievements. You can also successfully apply these techniques in the future if you need to. The use of the 'toolkit' we will construct in this section will help you to keep on track.

Lapse and relapse

When someone has beaten their worry, it is understandable they do not want it to become a problem again. This can mean they begin to look out for any signs that it is returning. They may misinterpret how they are feeling to indicate they are slipping into a relapse. It is important to remember it is normal for us all to experience worry at times. We cannot turn this off or remove it completely! We can also expect to experience more worry during times of stress, if we have ongoing pressure in our lives or specific upcoming events that are of concern. At such points, the amount of worry you experience may increase again. This is termed a 'lapse' – a temporary return of some symptoms. While this may be an increase in worry the same as anyone would experience in response to a difficult situation, you may then also worry that you are going to 'relapse' and your problem will take over again.

What is the difference between a lapse and a relapse?

A *lapse* is the brief return of some symptoms in a way that might interfere with your life. Lapses are normal and occur occasionally. So long as you put into practice the key principles of worry management, you can quickly get back on track again. It is important to see a lapse for what it is: just a temporary 'blip'. What is important is to remember that you already have the skills and knowledge you need to address this lapse.

Once you notice you are experiencing problematic worry, starting to use the techniques again (or increasing how much you are using them if you are already continuing their use) can prevent the re-occurrence of your vicious cycle of worry. Try to ensure you can still differentiate between practical worries and hypothetical worries. It may be that you have found ways to problem-solve without always using Worksheet 6 (page 194), but it might be useful to follow the structured work-sheet again if there has been an increase in your worries. You may also want to re-introduce scheduled worry time if you are experiencing problematic hypothetical worries. This will prevent a lapse becoming a relapse.

Don't give up. You know what works for you. Reapply the techniques you have learned and they will help again, just as returning to the gym after a break would allow you to regain your fitness. The use of the toolkit that we will construct in this section will help you to focus your efforts in doing this.

A *relapse* occurs when problematic worry returns over a longer period of time. The vicious cycle starts to spiral and the worry becomes even more problematic. The worry 'takes hold' and begins to significantly inter-fere with your enjoyment of life once again. If this happens, you still have the knowledge and skills to reapply worry management and recover. You know the principles of worry management and how the treatment works. The task of recovery is easier if you catch the problematic worry sooner, before excessive worry becomes ingrained in your life again – this is why it's really helpful to learn to notice the early warning signs that indicate things may be slipping backwards.

It is important to remember lapses may occur: stresses are inevitable, and you are likely to experience some problems with worry at such times. Recognise lapses for what they are and not as a sign that you have gone back to square one.

You have the tools to prevent a lapse from becoming a relapse. You know how to overcome your problem worry if it persists and the toolkit which you are about to construct will guide you in this. Try not to imagine a 'doomsday' scenario where all your problems suddenly reoccur at once. If there is some recurrence with problematic worry, it can feel like a fork in the road. According to which fork you take, you may either stay in control of your worry or slip back into the vicious cycle. You will tend to remain in control of your worry by:

- Keeping things in proportion and reminding yourself you are experiencing a 'blip' now, but overall things have been progressing

- Keeping in mind you have the tools to overcome any issues

- Maintaining the strategies you know help you that you have learned through this book

Of course you can go back through Section 3 at any point and reapply the techniques. This may increase your confidence and help you to get on top of your worry. However, the purpose of the toolkit we are about to construct is to help you focus in a more timely and efficient way on the key elements of that section, in order to get back on track more quickly.

Constructing your 'toolkit'

Hopefully, you will have learned from using this self-help book that techniques are available to help, and that these can continue to be put into action in the future if you feel the need to do so. Making a plan to maintain the gains that you have made (which I am referring to as a psychological 'toolkit' but is formally known as a 'relapse prevention plan') and then putting it into action as needed, reduces the likelihood that your problem worry will return. It will also ensure you have the confidence to spot any early warning signs.

You can think of this section as a toolkit to help you to:

- Regularly monitor your situation to keep on top of matters

- Recognise the circumstances that might lead you to start to worry excessively again

- Challenge beliefs that a return of some worry must indicate that your problematic worry is returning or that there is nothing you can do about this

- Put into place strategies to prevent a lapse from becoming a relapse

- Know where to get help and support in the future should you need it

My early warning signs

The first step in thinking about the future and dealing with any setbacks is to mentally make a note of the things you might notice when your worry begins to take hold. It can be helpful to spend some time thinking about this. These are the things that may indicate that difficulties are starting to return. If you notice them and take action, this may allow you to get on top of them before they begin to take hold and have an impact on your life.

Worksheet 10 (page 204) will help you to reflect on this. In it, write down the things you think you may experience that are the first signs of problems recurring. Think back to a time when your worry was first becoming a problem. Write down in the worksheet the changes you first noticed in the following:

- Your *behaviour*; what you did more or less of

- Your *thoughts*

- Your *feelings*

- The *physical feelings* in your body

To help you complete this task, you may want to turn back to the similar one you completed earlier (Worksheet 4). Are any of these symptoms relevant? Think back to the time when you first felt unwell, prior to the point when you decided to seek help.

It can also be helpful to speak to someone who knew you well over this period of time when problems were developing. Often, other people can start to see change before we notice it ourselves. They can have some really helpful observations. Perhaps they noticed you were starting to make some changes in what you were doing. Your sleep might have been impacted. It might be that you're starting to ask for reassurance about your worries again. Note down your most significant early warning signs on Worksheet 11 (page 205). These are the early indicators of a lapse that you need to look out for.

If you feel comfortable doing so, when you have completed it, share your toolkit with someone you are close to. If you or your loved ones notice the early warning signs are creeping back into your life, this is a good time to take action. You can use the principles of worry management in the same way you did before. If you have caught matters before they have slipped back too far, it should be more straightforward to regain the progress you previously made.

Therese had started to spend more time worrying again and working longer hours than she should. She realised she was slipping back into worry and its unhelpful behaviours (like the longer working hours). Therese decided to use a worry diary again to better understand the worries she was experiencing. She realised there were a number of practical worries about her finances that she was preoccupied with currently. The MOT was due on her car the following month and she was going to need to buy new school uniforms for the children soon. These had also triggered an increase in hypothetical worries about whether there might be something wrong with her car which would make the bill from the garage more expensive, or what if something went wrong with the house while she had these additional expenses. She saw that these hypothetical worries were related to the practical ones about finances. She made time to use the problem-solving technique again to address her practical worries. She decided to review her monthly budget, which she found helpful in recognising she was still managing to put some savings away each month. She was pleased to realise she could identify this solution. After she had successfully implemented this solution, she realised the hypothetical worries about her finances had also stopped. She felt more confident she could keep in control of her worries and use the different approaches if she ever needed them.

How things have improved since the start of treatment

Reflecting on what *you* have achieved is also an important part of your toolkit. This represents the power you have to overcome your problem with worry. Use Worksheet 12 (page 206) to list some of the improvements you have noticed since starting treatment. Reviewing your GAD-7 scores might help with this and also the content you completed earlier in terms of the impact of your worry on different aspects of your life. Changes might have happened in:

- Your relationships and social life (with your partner, family, friends and work colleagues)

- Work-life balance or ability to undertake other meaningful activities such as caring for others

- Ability to do essential things, whether housework, looking after children, or your own work

- Hobbies, whether things you do on our own or with others

In Section 1, I asked you to set some goals for yourself. You can now re-rate these by returning to Worksheet 3 (page 188). Review the progress you have made by comparing, for each of them, the first ratings of your goals to how you would rate them now. Sometimes, when change happens steadily, week by week, it's easy to lose track of all the progress you have made since the very start of the treatment. This should help you to get an overall sense of how much progress you have made.

Also, if you have not done so already, look back at the change in your GAD-7 scores by looking at your graph on Worksheet 1, page 186. (You can see the graphs for Therese and Mandeep in the recovery stories in Section 5). Compare where you were to where you are now. Have you managed to change the severity category for your symptoms? As I mentioned at the start of this book, generally speaking, health professionals will consider someone who scores below eight to have recovered.

Take a moment to reflect on how far you have come! Perhaps there are other things that have changed which I have not asked you about, but which are also important for you to note down?

What helped things to improve?

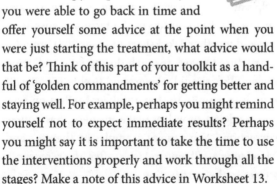

Which treatment techniques or strategies were particularly helpful to you in overcoming your problem worry? If you were able to go back in time and offer yourself some advice at the point when you were just starting the treatment, what advice would that be? Think of this part of your toolkit as a handful of 'golden commandments' for getting better and staying well. For example, perhaps you might remind yourself not to expect immediate results? Perhaps you might say it is important to take the time to use the interventions properly and work through all the stages? Make a note of this advice in Worksheet 13.

Now think about what advice you might tell yourself if you became aware of an early warning sign which could result in a lapse. Perhaps the advice might be quite similar to that which you have just noted above? Alternatively, it might be completely different. For example, you might say it is important to return to using your worry diary as soon as you become aware of the lapse. Now add this advice to Worksheet 13.

The wellbeing review

Another element of your toolkit is the completion of a regular 'wellbeing review'. Mark a day on your calendar each month, either physically or in your electronic diary, to prompt you to undertake this review. Having a review day will help you spot any early warning signs sooner and ensure you keep on top of the techniques we have covered together. Worksheet 14 (page 208) provides a structure to work through during your wellbeing review. This should take around twenty minutes. It is an opportunity to stop, think and reflect on how you are doing, as well as make any necessary 'course corrections'. You can see examples of Therese's and Mandeep's wellbeing reviews after their recovery stories in the next section.

If you are seeing a health professional to support you through this treatment, it is likely they will carry out at least one wellbeing review with you after you have finished treatment.

Is there anything else you would like to work on?

There may be alternative problems or issues you want to work on in the future. Perhaps you have noticed you experience some low mood when you are worried? Some of your goals may not be completely achieved yet. Are there any difficulties that are getting in the way of those? I would like to suggest it is worth noting these down in Worksheet 15. This is so you can remember them for later.

For the moment it is best to first focus on the difficulties that relate to your current goals. Focus on maintaining the progress you have made in regard to your worry. Once you have maintained this progress for a few months, you can return to any other item on this list. Depending on what remains, it may be that you can make use of this book again, or another one from the *How to Beat* series. The other books are structured very similarly to this one but contain different treatment strategies for different issues. If you have benefitted from using this book, you should cope very well with the others in the series.

If you are being supported by a health professional, they should be able to help you decide on how to move forward.

Relapse prevention top tips

Here are some top tips that might help you to use your toolkit to stay well:

1. The best way to prevent a lapse is to keep applying some of the underlying principles for recognising worries to maintain your control over them. Remember the fitness/exercise programme example? Just because you get in shape does not mean to say you should stop training. Within your monthly review, check you have routines in your life which help you maintain your worries in a 'normal' range. Also, check there are no practical worries which require you to use a problem-solving approach. Use the principles of worry management to get on top of your situation if you need to.

2. Learn your early warning signs. Watch out for times when you feel more

stressed or when there is a lot of change in your life. Perhaps work is very busy or there are changes happening at home. If you have shared your early warning signs with others, they may be able to notice early changes in your symptoms.

3. Complete a wellbeing review even if you have been feeling well. It will remind you to keep going with what has been successful. These don't have to be monthly. You may want to make them weekly or fortnightly to start with. When you feel more confident in maintaining your progress, you can then space the reviews out again.

4. Check that you haven't fallen back into any unhelpful patterns of worry. If you have, think about how you can apply your learning from worry time and problem-solving to get back to a place where your worries don't feel beyond your control.

5. Try not to be self-critical. Everyone worries at times and it is natural at such points to have concerns that you are slipping backwards. Focus on how you might stop a lapse from becoming a relapse.

6. If you need to revisit any of the worry management approaches again after you

have completed treatment, try not to see this as a step backwards. You may worry this is a sign that you will never get better. You could consider this as a practical worry, and this toolkit can be part of your action plan. Try rather to focus on how effective these approaches were for you before in reducing your symptoms. If they worked for you previously, they are likely to work for you again. Remember, maintaining good mental health relies on including these kinds of techniques generally in your life.

7.   Use your toolkit as often as you need to.

Getting further help if you need it

Sometimes, despite all of the hard work, you may still feel you require additional help. Knowing where and how to get help is an important final component of your toolkit. In the 'Further resources' section I have listed some organisations that may be able to support you. Let's have a think now about some of the people around you who can form part of your 'wellbeing team'.

Think of those around you who you
trust and who could support you.
Could you share your toolkit with
them so they can help you to watch
out for any early warning signs?
Having read your toolkit, they will also be aware of
what you might need in order to feel better. Perhaps
they can prompt you to access that? Write down on
Worksheet 16 (page 212) the name of anyone you
feel would be a good supporter in that role.

Your family doctor will usually be a key figure in
your support plan. You may have been seeing them
periodically throughout this treatment. If you need
support, remember they are there to offer medical
advice and they should also be able to refer you, as
needed, to other expert health professionals. Add
their details to Worksheet 16.

Finally on the worksheet, make a note of any organisations from the 'Further resources' section (or
elsewhere) that you may want to contact should you
need any other professional support. I would suggest you contact them when you are well and at your
best, just so you are sure they are the right people to
reach out to if you are having a lapse or relapse and
need additional support.

Congratulations!

We have come an awfully long way on this journey together. I am really pleased you have managed to complete worry management and get almost to the end of this book. Take a moment to think about the progress you've made towards your goals. The journey may not have been easy. The progress you've made is down to you – I've just provided you with some tools to allow you to help yourself. Hopefully, I've provided you with the hammer, wood and nails; you have built the table. With these tools, you can build other tables in the future. Be proud of what you have achieved. Perhaps you can apply some of these principles to other areas of your life to help you to achieve other goals? The problem-solving approach in particular can be especially helpful in lots of different areas of your life.

This relapse prevention section will help you maintain your progress. It will alert you when to put the necessary tools back into action if the need arises. This book will always be here if you need it again.

In the next section, we return to Therese's and Mandeep's stories. We have already seen how they used some of the aspects of worry management but they will let us know more broadly about how they used CBT self-help to get on top of their problem worry. Some people write down their own story for themselves in the way that Therese and Mandeep have told theirs. It is a reminder of what they have achieved. Others may write a short letter to themselves to celebrate their progress. If you think it might be helpful, perhaps you could write your own story in this kind of way after you recover? You could write it as if it were a letter to yourself in the future, like a time capsule. Pieces of writing like this can also be added to the toolkit if you wish. You can then re-read them as part of your wellbeing reviews, adding to them every so often if needed.

I have also provided you with blank worksheets and the details of some organisations that may be of help at the back of the book. You should now have all the tools you need to keep your worry in check in the future. I wish you well.

RECOVERY STORIES

Therese's story

You met Therese on pages 41–4 and have seen some aspects of her use of worry management in Section 3. Her problems with worry had been getting worse since her ex-partner started a new relationship. Worry was impacting her relationship with her children, who she was being much stricter with in terms of what they were allowed to do and where they were allowed to go. It was impacting her work, as she was worrying a lot about how well she was performing and finding the workload unmanageable. It was also affecting her relationships with her friends as her worries were resulting in her not seeing them as often. This was because she was worried that she did not have the money to socialise and because she was bringing work home with her and spending some of her evenings attending to that. She has used worry management to help her overcome these difficulties. This is her recovery story.

" I would say that I've always been a bit of a worrier, but this last twelve months it has got much worse than it has ever been before. I started to feel like all I ever did was worry. The first thoughts that entered my head in the morning were worries. They were often in my head when I was trying to go to sleep at night as well. I split up from my partner Sam three years ago and I've probably been worrying a bit more since then. Although Sam does still help me financially and helps with the kids as well, it feels like a lot more responsibility sits with me now. I struggle to stop the worries coming into my head about what might happen if I lost my job, or there was a problem with my house or car that I couldn't afford to fix. The more I think about things, the more other worries come into my head. It's like a spiral that I just can't stop going down. It has made me more determined to do my work as well as I possibly can to make sure that I keep my job. Now I've noticed I'm working longer and longer hours, double and triple-checking my work to make sure I've got it all right!

Over the last couple of months, my kids (aged twelve and fourteen) have been complaining that I'm not letting them do as many things. They've got friends who live a couple of streets away and I used to let them walk over there together. Recently I keep worrying that something bad might happen so I'll only let them go if I can walk with them or if their friend's mum comes and picks them up. I know it isn't fair on them but I just can't stop these worries coming into my head about what might happen!

My mum said that I worried a lot as a teenager as well, especially when it was coming up to exams. I don't really remember it much but Mum said I'd stay up really late revising and would talk to her about all my worries. She said she didn't really know how to help me but I got some support from the school nurse and it seemed to get better once I finished my exams.

A friend called me up recently to see how I was. She said she was concerned because I hadn't gone along to the last few meet-ups with our friends. In the end

I explained a bit about how I had been feeling and how difficult the worries had become for me. I was really embarrassed to tell her but she was so lovely about it. She told me that her sister-in-law had a similar issue recently and had found this book that had really helped her called *How to Beat Worry*. She said she'd get a copy for me which I was so grateful for. I quite liked the idea of trying to use a book as I didn't really know whether it was something I could go to the doctor about. I didn't want to have to take time off work or tell my manager so I was really hopeful this was going to be useful. My friend also said she'd be happy to help me and talk to me about it as much as I wanted her to. I knew I could talk to my mum as well.

I couldn't wait to get started reading the book. I was a bit nervous about how hard it might be but I knew I needed to make some changes before things got any worse. I read the first two chapters really quickly. I then decided I needed to slow down a bit and set aside some proper time to do the different tasks the book was suggesting. I went back to the beginning, and this time made sure to do each of the activities the book recommended. I found that really helpful as the parts I'd been a bit unsure about started making more sense as I read through the book again.

I found it especially helpful to complete the GAD-7, an easy questionnaire to complete which consists of seven questions about my worry, as it really made me realise just how much my worries were having an impact on my life. I've made a really conscious effort to complete this every week. It has been so helpful to see the changes, even when sometimes things didn't change or went up a little bit. I could normally understand the result because of the things that had been going on that week for me.

I decided I would also tell my children about using the book and doing the different activities to try and help my worry. I didn't want to upset them but I knew they had noticed I 'wasn't myself'. I thought it would be useful for them to know I was trying to do something about it. They had already noticed the book on my bedside table and really encouraged me to give it a go. They were really lovely about it and every so often would ask me how I was getting on with it.

The other thing I found really helpful about starting the book was knowing that this was a normal problem that lots of other people struggled with as well. At points over the last few months I'd started to think I might be going mad and that there was something really wrong with me. It was a big relief to know that I wasn't the only person to have these problems and that there was proper research which proved that I could get better – and that I could learn how to do this myself.

I was really apprehensive about actually starting the work. I knew I needed to do it. I decided to copy some of the worksheets so I could have some extras rather than just write them in the book. Writing down my worries in a worry diary was really easy at first because there were just so many of them! I did it once a day for a few days. I wrote enough to fill three worksheets. It got a bit harder when I was trying to categorise them though. Initially I felt like everything was practical. These kinds of worries were often about my finances and how important my job is to pay me enough money to look after my kids. They all felt so real to me. I forced myself to really think about each one though. I started to realise that some of them were much more hypothetical. They were often more about things that could potentially go wrong but were not definitely going to happen. Often they would relate back to one particular practical worry, but then my brain would run away with itself and the 'what if' worries would spiral and spiral. One of the worries I often had was that I didn't have enough money in savings for if something went wrong with the car or the house. This then led to other worries about the risk of losing my job, or something more and more

dramatic going wrong with the house. When I realised that it was often a practical worry that started
these thoughts, I decided that it would make sense
to start with problem-solving – a system to method-
ically come up with an action plan to solve practical
worries – and see if that made any difference.

At first, I was unsure how helpful I would find the
problem-solving. I'm a single working mum with
two children so I feel like I already spend a lot of
time solving problems – both my own and other
people's! Often friends will come to me for advice
about what they should do about this situation or
that problem. I thought I should already know how
to do it so really was it going to make that much of a
difference? I had promised myself I would properly
give it a go though, so that's what I did. I talked to
my mum about which of the practical worries I
should start with. It was helpful to talk the different
ones through with her to feel more confident that it
definitely was a practical worry that I could use. It
seemed to help that Mum was much more confident
about what a practical worry was. We spent some
time thinking about how to word it on the worksheet to make sure it was really clear. [You can see
the content of Therese's problem-solving on page
87.] We then started trying to come up with solutions. At first I found it really hard, but doing it with
Mum really helped and in the end we had a bit of a

giggle coming up with some really daft solutions as well. I also found it really helpful to say to myself, 'If a friend was having this worry what would I suggest?' Somehow removing myself from the situation helped me think more clearly about it. It felt good to channel my energy into solving a problem rather than just worrying about it. The next time I used problem-solving though I forced myself to do it on my own as I wanted to make sure that I didn't become reliant on Mum or get her to do it for me. I decided to try and do the next stage of picking the right solution myself even the very first time I did it. Most of the time I found it quite straightforward to pick the right solution to try. Sometimes though there were two or three that might be okay, so that took a bit longer to think about. I went back to the pros and cons of each of them a few times before picking one.

I found it really helpful to plan exactly how I was going to carry out the solution. I guess it makes sense looking back now but before I thought I should just know how to do it and it shouldn't be that hard. Taking that time to work through all the different stages and thinking about what I might need to make it work made me feel more confident about actually doing it. Being really specific about when and where I was going to be helped me to do it when I was feeling worried or nervous about it as well.

At the end of the process you produce an action plan. This is a detailed step-by-step plan of exactly how you are going to try to solve the problem. The first time I put my action plan into place I felt really nervous about how it would go, but because I'd spent time planning it, it worked really well! I couldn't believe how successful it was and what a relief it was to solve the problem! The action plan was about remembering to take work back to school with me which I had brought home the night before [you can see the full detail of this is in the problem-solving stage in Section 3]. Part of me was annoyed at myself for needing to use the process. I wrote this down as part of my review. It was useful to remind myself what the book had already told me, that when I was feeling better I would be able to do it for myself again but, right now, because my worries had become problematic, I needed to use this strategy.

I managed to use the problem-solving three times that first week, and was really pleased I'd been able to make some changes. The first time was about my worry of forgetting to take work back to the school office with me. The second time it was in relation to a worry about my kids going to their friend's house for a sleepover at the weekend. The third time was about my car needing its service and MOT next month and how I was going to be able to afford this.

I was continuing to keep the worry diary as well. I noticed that the number of hypothetical worries was reducing too because they were often connected to a practical worry. So once I had fixed the practical worry, the hypothetical ones seemed to just not happen as much! This was especially useful when I was worrying about my kids going to the sleepover. I decided to talk to them about my worry a bit – I told them how much I would miss them and might worry whether they were doing okay and enjoying themselves. I didn't share all my worries because I didn't want them to also start worrying about bad things happening to them but once I had come up with some different solutions in Stage 3 I shared the list with them and we went through the pros and cons together. We agreed together which was the best solution: I could text them a maximum of twice in the evening and if I did they would reply to me. They also agreed that if they forgot to reply I could text the friend's mum to check in on them. This worked really well and in the end I managed to only send them a text message once – and they did reply to me. I decided I'd keep going with the problem-solving for at least another week before trying the worry time as I felt like I was making good progress.

One night, about three weeks in, I had a really bad evening of worrying. I'd had a message from my ex-partner Sam earlier that day to tell me they were moving in with their new girlfriend. They said they'd be happy to arrange a time to speak about it and tried to reassure me that nothing was going to change in terms of the kids, but I couldn't help but worry. That night I slept really badly and kept waking up with worries going around my head. I decided to fill in a worry diary the next day. This time there were a lot more hypothetical worries. What if Sam didn't want the kids staying over anymore? What if they didn't like Sam's new girlfriend? What if Sam's girlfriend didn't like them or didn't know how to look after them properly? What if they really liked Sam's new girlfriend and wanted to spend less time with me!? I decided to have a proper look at worry time again and give it a go.

I had already read about it in the book but, as it had been a few weeks ago, I read through it again. I started to follow the steps. That day, I used the notes app on my phone and listed all the worries I was having as they came into my head. It was really hard to then try to re-focus my attention. I don't think I managed it perfectly, but I kept telling myself 'it's already written down' when it came back into my head. A few times I started singing 'Let It Go' – which I knew really well from when the kids were little – which helped me more than I expected because it also made me laugh, and sometimes the kids joined in singing when I was at home with them. I definitely managed to focus on my work more than I normally would when I was worrying.

That evening I had decided I was going to do my worry time at 6.30 p.m. The kids had gone round to their friends' for tea. I was picking them up at 7.30 p.m. so that gave me twenty minutes for worry time, a bit of time afterwards to review it and get my head together for picking them up later. It felt really strange to just sit there and look at my list of worries and *allow* myself to worry about them. I felt a bit silly at times. When I read through some of the worries, it made me think they were silly as well. Especially the one about the kids not wanting to spend as much time with me. However exciting the new girlfriend was I knew really that would never happen. I was able to cross a few of them out as I didn't feel bothered about them anymore. There were others that did still feel important, but reading them again I knew I couldn't do anything about them, so I left them on the list so I could think about them in my next worry time.

I was glad I'd given myself the extra time to review how it felt afterwards – that really helped me to think a bit about the whole process. I noticed that even though I hadn't really done anything, I had managed to reduce some of my worries and I felt less distressed about some of the others. I had gone into the exercise quite sceptical so I was surprised to realise it had helped.

I made the decision that I would keep trying with the worry time over the next week to see how I got on with it. I still found it a bit strange to just sit and stare at the list of worries. I did start to get more used to it and, nearly every time, I was able to cross off at least one or two worries. A couple of times I also identified that one of the worries was practical. I was then able to put it on the top of a problem-solving worksheet, cross it out, then do some problem-solving with it the next day. After about a week, I decided to reduce the amount of worry time down to fifteen minutes after I realised I was finishing sooner than the twenty minutes I'd allocated to it.

It has been about two months now since I started using the book and I've definitely noticed a difference. I've managed to address a number of really practical things. I've done myself a monthly budget so I feel more confident about how much money I've got. I've talked to my boss about my work and she did an appraisal review with me. Although I was nervous going into it, I had prepared for the meeting and it went really well. This has helped me to feel more secure at work, and also my boss now understands a bit more about my worry, which I also talked about in the appraisal. I think it is helpful for her to know so she can better understand if I start worrying more again. Having done these things has really taken some pressure off me, and while I am still worried about things, I feel like they are much more like the type of worries I normally have and I definitely feel more in control of them. The kids have noticed a difference as well – especially as I've started letting them go to their friends' house on their own, as long as they let me know when they get there!"

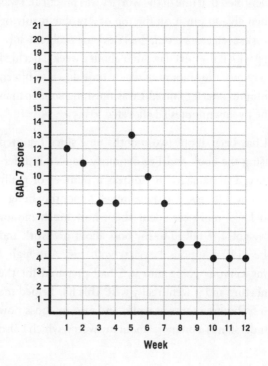

Therese's Wellbeing Review

Review date: 18th June

What have my symptoms been like over the last month?

Most of the time I haven't noticed any symptoms at all. Sometimes if I have a lot of work to get through I can start to worry about it, but I seem to be noticing this sooner and taking time to plan how I'm going to tackle the work. I was worried when my eldest went on a school residential a couple of weeks ago – but lots of the other mums said they were worried too, and as soon as she was home and I knew what a good time she'd had (and that she was okay!) it just seemed to go away again.

Any new activities that have helped me progress to my goals?

I have gone back to seeing my friends every month again and haven't missed a get-together for a while. I am still using the problem-solving regularly particularly at work and finding this helpful.

Reading through my early warning signs (Worksheet 10), have I had any experiences that have concerned me?

I am doing well at sticking to my working hours – I know when I start working late it is a sign I'm starting to struggle. I am also sleeping well at the minute which I know is a good sign.

Do I need to take any actions now to keep on top of my worry?

I don't think I need any new actions, but do need to keep using the things that are working for me and keep seeing my friends regularly.

If so, what will be helpful to use (refer to Worksheet 13 and also 'relapse prevention top tips' in this book)?

Nothing at the moment

What do I need to do and when am I going to do it?

Nothing currently but will review again next month

My GAD-7 score is: 2

The date of my next review is: 18th July 2024

Mandeep's story

You met Mandeep on pages 45–7 and have seen some aspects of his engagement with worry management in Section 3 when he used worry time (pages 110–11). Mandeep is in his first year of a chemical engineering degree and has begun to struggle with problematic worry. This is largely related to being a student, but also in terms of his family responsibilities, ambitions for the future and also his relationships with his peers. As Mandeep was getting closer to his end-of-year exams he was finding these worries increasingly difficult. He has used worry management to help overcome these difficulties. This is his recovery story.

"I wouldn't have described myself as a worrier before but moving away from home to come to university felt like a really big deal. I've always been really close to my family. Being the eldest son it was a big thing when I said I was going to move away to go to university. I didn't get into my first choice of university where I could have attended while living at home. Because this course was really important to me I accepted the offer of my second choice of university which meant I had to move out as it is further away. Since I've got here, I've found things really hard. I think not getting into my first choice of university knocked my confidence. I'm worried I'm not really keeping up with the coursework. It is so different from being in college and there are some *really* clever people here! There are things I really like; I've made a group of good friends on the same course and I do still really enjoy the subject. I'm just starting to worry I'm not good enough to be here. I've been preparing for end-of-term exams and that has been making me more worried. I'm going to have my first placement next year. I've never worked in a role like that before and I really don't know what to expect.

University life is so different from when I was living at home. My faith has always been a big part of my life and I have tried to keep up with it here but all the changes in routine are making it hard. I don't really know anyone else who is Hindu here so that feels weird too. My friends on the course do work hard but they also spend a lot of time in the student union bar and on nights out at the local pubs. They always invite me along, but I don't drink and have never really felt that comfortable in pubs and bars. That's just not what I have ever done with my friends back home. I worry my parents would think badly of me if I started going out more. However, I also don't want my university friends to stop making an effort to hang out with me if I always turn down their invites for a night out or a Sunday afternoon in the pub. It's made me worried about my future in other ways as well. Most of them have been on dates since we got here. A couple have got girlfriends now. I don't really get much opportunity to talk to girls. Certainly not girls that my family would approve of as a potential future wife. I know I'm only young but there is a lot of expectation on me as the eldest boy to marry the right person, so it does prey on my mind a lot.

There have been a few times when I've been so overwhelmed with all the worries about everything, I've ended up cutting myself with an old razorblade. I don't really know where the idea came from, but the physical sensation of the blade on my skin just forced me to think about that instead of the worries. They've never been bad cuts, they've never even needed a plaster and usually don't break the skin, but I definitely don't want to keep doing it.

I had a meeting with my personal tutor a few weeks ago. It was the third time I'd met them. I like them so I decided to be brave and tell them how I've been feeling. I was worried about how they would respond. That they would tell me I need to change my degree. They were actually really supportive. They gave me some information about different support options I could access, including a student wellbeing service. They also recommended a book called *How to Beat Worry* that they knew a couple of other previous students had found helpful when they were experiencing similar kinds of problems. I had a chat with my sister about it that night on a video call – she and I have always been close and she's the one person in the family I've been able to talk to about this. I said I wasn't sure how comfortable I felt going to talk to someone in student wellbeing. She said that was silly because the whole point of the service was so people could talk to them, but she encouraged me to get the book from the library and give the treatment a go. I decided I would try this first and if I didn't like it then I might consider going to the student wellbeing service. My sister said she'd be happy to talk to me again on a video call and help with any of it if I needed. She even offered to come and visit me if that would help.

I was worried about how I was going to find time to use the book when I had so much work to do for my studies. I know I'm not really being that productive at the minute. Whenever I sit down to try and revise I'm really struggling to concentrate. Then my brain just starts focusing on all these worries instead. So I decided I would try and make just a bit of time every day to try and start working through the book and see if it helped.

I found the structure of the book really helped me to just do a bit at a time and I felt better the first time I did the GAD-7 as it made me realise I wasn't as bad as I thought! It was useful to know this was a real problem other people experienced too. I could really identify with the vicious cycle of worry and how stuck I had got in it. This made me feel hopeful that the book was going to be able to help me.

I found keeping the worry diary quite difficult as worries would just pop into my head at all kinds of random times. In the end I started keeping a record of them on my phone initially, then I could write them down whenever they happened. This was also less obvious to other people: I hadn't told any of my university friends about the treatment. I found writing them down a bit strange. Seeing them on the screen made me feel silly for thinking some of them, but at the same time I couldn't stop them!

When it came to categorising the worries I first copied the worries from my phone onto one of the worry diaries in the book. I had in my head that most of them were going to be practical and current because so many were about the course. I even tried to do problem-solving with one of them, but it just didn't work as well as I hoped because there weren't really any solutions – it depended on other things happening first. I got really stuck trying to find a solution to 'what if no one ever wants to marry me?' [You can see more examples of Mandeep's worries on page 110]. I also got quite upset when I was spending so much time trying to think of solutions and not coming up with any.

In the end I talked to my sister about it. I felt really embarrassed but she helped me to realise that really this was a hypothetical worry and there wasn't any-thing I could do about it now – other than try and keep being friendly and talking to girls! With one of the worries though I did manage to find solu-tions which took the form of 'if that happens this is what I'll do'. This was concerning failing any of my exams. After using the problem-solving process, the solution I chose was to talk to my tutor about what would happen if I did fail any of them. This really helped as they explained that I would always get a second opportunity to sit an exam. They also talked to me about some revision tips which really helped. This did make me feel a bit better, know-ing I had a plan of how I would tackle something if it happened. It made me realise how many of my worries were actually hypothetical though! [You can see an example of one of Mandeep's completed worry diaries in the worry time section in Section 3, page 104 onwards]. That in itself was so useful to realise because I had been convinced that I should have been doing more but just didn't know what.

So then I realised I needed to give the worry time a go. I did feel a bit apprehensive about it – I'm not sure I really understood why giving myself time to worry would be helpful, but I'd promised my sister I would try it and figured that it couldn't make it any worse. I decided the best time for me to do this was 9 p.m. – I always go to bed later and I thought I would try and do it after my revision to help me not study too late into the night which had been becoming more common.

Similarly to how I had recorded the worries to put into my worry diary, I just used my phone to record all my worries in the notes app. I surprised myself that, once I'd written them down, I found it quite easy to re-focus my attention. I could just say to myself 'it is written down now' and it really made a difference to keeping my focus on what I was supposed to be doing, knowing I could think about the worries again later.

Once I got to the worry time, I put my phone on airplane mode so I wouldn't have any distractions. I decided to plan thirty minutes as my list of worries seemed to be very long. It did feel a bit strange to be allowed time to just sit and look at them and think about them. Knowing I was allowed to cross some out though was really helpful because when I started reading through them, some of them seemed so unlikely or so far away in the future that I felt happy to cross them out. This meant that the list was a lot shorter by the end of the worry time.

I actually stopped after about twenty minutes. It didn't feel useful to continue for any longer that evening. Like the book suggested, I took some time afterwards to reflect on how I had found the process and was surprised that it did seem like it had been more useful than I had expected it to be. It made me quite excited about doing it the next day because I was hopeful that I would have a more productive day again because I would be able to write them down and then re-focus my attention. I had sometimes thought that my worrying was going to help me work really hard for my degree, but actually now I realised that the worry was really getting in the way of my work. By focusing on the content of my revision for my exams, instead of worrying whether or not I would be successful in them, I was definitely being more productive. I also slept better that night and even though I hadn't technically revised for as long that evening, I actually felt like I had learned more because I had been able to focus more.

I've been using worry time for about a month now and have been amazed at what a difference it has made to me. I'm still writing my worries down, but I've started doing worry time every other day and only for fifteen minutes. I think that it is writing them down and being able to re-focus my attention which is making the most difference to me. I'm really pleased with the preparation I've been able to do for my exams and I'm starting to feel more confident that I am going to be able to pass them!

The worries about my future haven't gone away completely but because I'm writing them down now, when I do take time to look at them properly I can recognise that I probably don't need to worry about them too much yet. There are still so many things that could change and influence what happens. I'm trying my best not to let my worries spiral away from me and for the most part it is working well now.

I've also not been using the razorblade at all. I made a decision to try to not do it when I started working through the book, but actually I haven't even thought about it so I'm hopeful I'm not going to do that again.

I had another meeting with my personal tutor last week. I talked to them about how I had been using the book and the difference it was making. They were really encouraging and pleased I had made such good progress. I was now feeling more confident with the course as well."

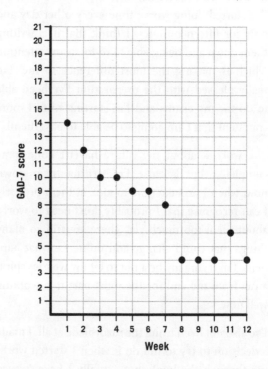

Mandeep's Wellbeing Review

Review date: 2nd September

What have my symptoms been like over the last month?

It has been a good month where I have felt really good. I've been back living with my family over summer and enjoying being back at home and around my old friends.

Any new activities that have helped me progress to my goals?

Nothing new but being back at home spending time with my friends and working at my old job has felt really good and I've definitely noticed I'm more relaxed.

Reading through my early warning signs (Worksheet 10), have I had any experiences that have concerned me?

The last couple of weeks I've started thinking more about going back to university and especially about the placement I'll start in the New Year. Occasionally I've found myself worrying about what it will be like. I've not slept as well this last week.

Do I need to take any actions now to keep on top of my worry?

Yes. I have started noticing worries again so think it might be useful to start writing them down again.

If so, what will be helpful to use (refer to Worksheet 13 and also 'relapse prevention top tips' in this book)?

I need to categorise my worries to decide what will be helpful and if there are any practical things I can do. I know most of them are hypothetical as are mainly related to my placement – I don't even know where this will be yet and doesn't start until January.

What do I need to do and when am I going to do it?

I will start writing my worries down today and categorise them this evening. I will then try problem-solving if there are practical worries, and also start worry time tomorrow evening.

My GAD-7 score is: 6

The date of my next review is: 2nd Oct. 2024

WORKBOOK

Notes

Use this page to record page numbers and notes that are linked to the key points that you may want to refer back to, either while you are using the book or in the future.

_____

_____

_____

_____

_____

_____

_____

_____

_____

_____

_____

_____

_____

_____

_____

_____

_____

_____

_____

_____

_____

_____

_____

_____

_____

_____

_____

_____

_____

_____

_____

_____

_____

_____

_____

_____

_____

_____

_____

_____

_____

_____

_____

_____

_____

_____

_____

_____

_____

_____

_____

_____

_____

_____

_____

_____

_____

_____

_____

_____

_____

_____

_____

_____

_____

_____

_____

Worksheet 1: Weekly record of GAD-7 score

Date	GAD-7 score

Graph for plotting GAD-7 score progress

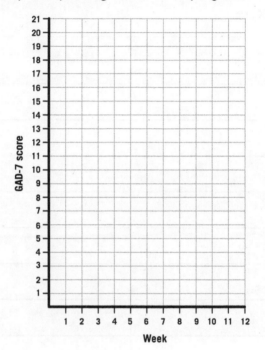

Worksheet 2: Making change happen

How important is it for me to change?

Do I have the opportunity to change?

Worksheet 3: My goals

Goal 1: ....

....

....

I can do this now   (Today's date___/___/___)
(circle a number):

0	1	2	3	4	5	6
Not at all		Occasionally		Often		Any time

One month re-rating   (date___/___/___)
(circle a number):

0	1	2	3	4	5	6
Not at all		Occasionally		Often		Any time

Two month re-rating   (date___/___/___)
(circle a number):

0	1	2	3	4	5	6
Not at all		Occasionally		Often		Any time

Three month re-rating   (date___/___/___)
(circle a number):

0	1	2	3	4	5	6
Not at all		Occasionally		Often		Any time

Goal 2: ....

....

....

I can do this now   (Today's date___/___/___)
(circle a number):

    0   1   2   3   4   5   6

  Not at all   Occasionally   Often   Any time

One month re-rating   (date___/___/___)
(circle a number):

    0   1   2   3   4   5   6

  Not at all   Occasionally   Often   Any time

Two month re-rating   (date___/___/___)
(circle a number):

    0   1   2   3   4   5   6

  Not at all   Occasionally   Often   Any time

Three month re-rating   (date___/___/___)
(circle a number):

    0   1   2   3   4   5   6

  Not at all   Occasionally   Often   Any time

Goal 3: ....

....

....

I can do this now   (Today's date___/___/___)
(circle a number):

0	1	2	3	4	5	6
Not at all		Occasionally		Often		Any time

One month re-rating   (date___/___/___)
(circle a number):

0	1	2	3	4	5	6
Not at all		Occasionally		Often		Any time

Two month re-rating   (date___/___/___)
(circle a number):

0	1	2	3	4	5	6
Not at all		Occasionally		Often		Any time

Three month re-rating   (date___/___/___)
(circle a number):

0	1	2	3	4	5	6
Not at all		Occasionally		Often		Any time

Worksheet 4: How is your worry affecting you?

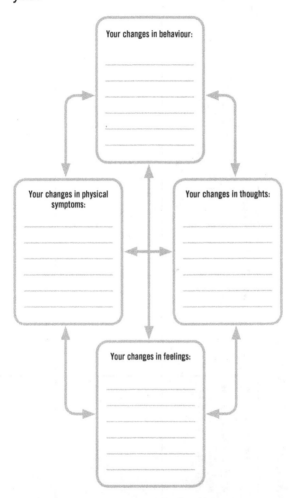

Worksheet 5: Worry diary

Situation What am I doing, where am I, who am I with and what is happening when the worry occurs?	What is the worry?	How anxious am I feeling? Rate from 0 to 10 0 = not anxious 10 = most anxious ever felt	What type of worry am I having?	
			Hypothetical (H)	Practical (P)

Worksheet 6: Problem-solving

Stage 1: Identify the worry

_____

_____

_____

Stage 2: Identify solutions

1. _____
2. _____
3. _____
4. _____
5. _____
6. _____
7. _____
8. _____

Stage 3: Assess the strengths and weaknesses of each potential solution

You can use Worksheet 7 for this stage

Stage 4: Choosing a solution

Chosen solution

_____

_____

Other 'maybe' solutions

_____

_____

Stage 5: Planning the solution

Step 1: _____

_____

_____

_____

Step 2: _____

_____

_____

_____

Step 3: _____

_____

_____

Step 4: _____

_____

_____

Stage 6: Trying the solution

Stage 7: Reviewing how it went

_____

_____

_____

_____

_____

_____

_____

_____

Worksheet 7: Strengths and weaknesses

Solution 1:	
Strengths:	Weaknesses:

Solution 2:	
Strengths:	Weaknesses:

Solution 3:	
Strengths:	Weaknesses:

Solution 4:	
Strengths:	Weaknesses:

Solution 5:

Strengths:	Weaknesses:

Solution 6:

Strengths:	Weaknesses:

Solution 7:

Strengths: Weaknesses:

Solution 8:

Strengths: Weaknesses:

Worksheet 8: Worry time list

Use this worksheet to record your worries through the day. You will then focus on this list during worry time. If the worry occurs more than once, you can keep a tally of how often you experience the same worry.

When you use this list during worry time, if there are worries where the associated anxiety rating has changed, you can alter these. If there are worries which no longer bother you, you can put a line through them.

My worry time schedule:		
Worry	Anxiety rating	Tally

Worksheet 9: Worry time review

_____

_____

_____

_____

_____

_____

_____

_____

_____

_____

_____

_____

_____

_____

_____

_____

_____

_____

_____

Worksheet 10: My early warning signs

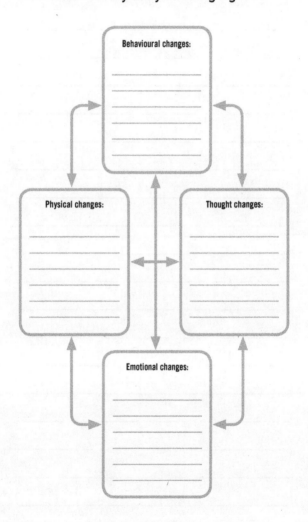

Worksheet 11: My most significant early warning signs

_____

_____

_____

_____

_____

_____

_____

_____

_____

_____

_____

_____

_____

_____

_____

_____

_____

_____

_____

_____

Worksheet 12: Positive improvements achieved over treatment

Worksheet 13: Things that helped me
achieve improvements

_____

_____

_____

_____

_____

_____

_____

_____

_____

_____

_____

_____

_____

_____

_____

_____

_____

_____

Worksheet 14: Wellbeing review

Review date:
What have my symptoms been like over the last month?
Any new activities that have helped me progress to my goals?
Reading through my early warning signs (Worksheet 10), have I had any experiences that have concerned me?

Do I need to take any actions now to keep on top of my worry?

If so, what will be helpful to use (refer to Worksheet 13 and also 'relapse prevention top tips' in this book)?

What do I need to do and when am I going to do it?

My GAD-7 score is:

The date of my next review is:

Worksheet 15: Issue(s) to work on in the future

What do you still want to work on?

At this point, do you have any ideas how you will do this?

When do you plan to do it (perhaps add in a reminder on your calendar)?

Are there any resources that you need to get hold of to help with this?

Are there any things that might get in the way of you working on this, and how might you overcome these?

Worksheet 16: Useful sources of support

_____

_____

_____

_____

_____

_____

_____

_____

_____

_____

_____

_____

_____

_____

_____

_____

_____

_____

FURTHER RESOURCES

Generalised anxiety disorder and worry

- The UK NHS website has a summary of useful information about generalised anxiety disorder, including different treatment options and a helpful video. The webpage is: https://www.nhs.uk/mental-health/conditions/generalised-anxiety-disorder/overview

- The World Health Organization also provides helpful information about anxiety disorders, including key facts and self-care information. The webpage is: https://www.who.int/news-room/fact-sheets/detail/anxiety-disorders

- Anxiety UK is a charity organisation. Their website provides helpful information on what anxiety is and links to useful resources. Other information about what the organisation can offer is available here: https://www.anxietyuk.

org.uk/anxiety-type/generalised-anxiety-disorder

- The Better Health: Every Mind Matters website is an NHS resource which provides wellbeing tips on a range of different issues. Their page on tackling worries is available here: https://www.nhs.uk/every-mind-matters/mental-wellbeing-tips/self-help-cbt-techniques/tackling-your-worries

NHS Talking Therapies for Anxiety and Depression

- NHS Talking Therapies are an England-based service. The website provides an overview of different problems the service can help with and links to find your local service: https://www.nhs.uk/mental-health/talking-therapies-medicine-treatments/talking-therapies-and-counselling/nhs-talking-therapies

Panic attack resources

- The UK NHS website also has a summary of useful information about panic attacks: https://www.nhs.uk/mental-health/conditions/panic-disorder

- Mind is a UK-based charitable organisation which campaigns for help and support for all people experiencing mental health problems. Their webpages contain useful information about panic attacks: https://www.mind.org.uk/information-support/types-of-mental-health-problems/anxiety-and-panic-attacks/panic-attacks

Relaxation exercises

- The Mind website also provides information on relaxation exercises which may be useful: https://www.mind.org.uk/information-support/tips-for-everyday-living/relaxation/relaxation-exercises

- The NHS website also includes an overview of breathing exercises for stress which you may find useful: https://www.nhs.uk/mental-health/self-help/guides-tools-and-activities/breathing-exercises-for-stress

- Harvard Medical School provides health information on common conditions. The following webpage describes six relaxation techniques to reduce stress: https://www.health.harvard.edu/mind-and-mood/six-relaxation-techniques-to-reduce-stress

Support for suicidal thoughts and thoughts of self-harm

- The notOK app is a free digital panic button to get you immediate support via text, phone call or GPS location if you are struggling to reach out: https://www.notokapp.com

- The Stay Alive app is a similar UK-based resource with useful information to help people experiencing thoughts of suicide or worried about someone else who is considering suicide: https://prevent-suicide.org.uk/find-help-now/stay-alive-app

- The Mind website provides information on crisis services and how to access them. There are also links to emergency advice: www.mind.org.uk/information-support/guides-to-support-and-services/crisis-services/crisis-teams-crhts

ACKNOWLEDGEMENTS

CBT self-help books have been published for several decades and health professionals have been supporting people in their use over this time. However, Dave Richards and Mark Whyte first published information about 'low intensity CBT' and the new role of the PWP in the English NHS.

A number of authors have created problem-solving worksheets. I have drawn heavily upon these, including:

Farrand, P., Woodford, J. and Small, F. (2019), *Managing Your Worries*. University of Exeter: CEDAR.

Richards, D. A. and Whyte, M. (2011), *Reach Out: National Programme Student Materials to Support the Delivery of Training for Psychological Wellbeing Practitioners Delivering Low Intensity Interventions* (3rd Edition). London: Rethink Mental Illness.

Aside from the editorial team at Little, Brown, Mark Papworth has commented on a draft of this book.

I would also like to thank my husband for his comments, proofreading skills and support in my writing of this book.

INDEX

Note: page numbers in *italics* refer to information contained in tables/worksheets, page numbers in **bold** refer to diagrams.

achievement, focus on 29
action-taking 25
activities of daily living 142
ancestors 58
anxiety 5, 6, 38, 44, 128
anxiety disorders 3–10, 58, 70
    see also generalised anxiety disorder
Anxiety UK 213–14
attention, re-focusing your 112–14, 124–5, 163, 177
avoidance behaviours 4, 128

'bad' days 27, 34
behaviour
    avoidance behaviours 4, 128

changes in **39**, 41–3, 46–7, **62–3**, **66**, 105, **120**, **191**, **204**
and worry 38–9, **39**, 41–3, 46–7, **56–7**, 61, 64, **66**, 83, 105, **120**, 128, 139
belief *see* self-beliefs
Better Health: Every Mind Matters, The (website) 214

case examples 19
    see also Mandeep; Therese
CBT self-help 16, 44, 48, 150
    efficacy 59
    and 'feeling like giving up' 30–1

getting support with
  30–1, 32–3
how the book works
  17–23
and note-making
  18–19, 26–7
pace of 15
and progress reviews
  29–30, 141–3, *206*
scheduling time for 29
and taking small steps
  31
top tips for 23–30
see also worry
  management
  interventions
challenges 24, 41
change
  behavioural **39**, 41–3,
    46–7, **62–3**, **66**, 105,
    120, **191**, **204**
  emotional **39**, **62–3**,
    66, **120**, **191**,
    204
  importance of 32
  making it happen
    31–3, 65, 67, *187*
  opportunities for 32–3
  physical 38, **39**, 42, 46,
    62–3, 65, **66**, 105,
    120, **191**, **204**
  and thoughts **39**,
    41–3, 45–7, **62–3**,
    65, **66**, 105, **120**,
    191, **204**

cognitive behavioural
  therapy (CBT) 14–15,
  38–9, **39**, 65
  efficacy 59
  high intensity 15
  low intensity 15
  see also CBT self-
    help; relapse
    prevention toolkit;
    worry management
    interventions
compassion 30
concentration difficulties
  3, 5, 46
control issues 52

daily living, activities of
  142
depression, comorbidity
  with generalised anxiety
  disorder 8–9
distraction techniques 47
'doomsday' scenarios 136

early warning signs
  My early warning
    signs worksheet
    138–9, **204**
  My most significant
    early warning signs
    worksheet *205*
  and relapse prevention
    135, 138–41, 144,
    146–7, 149, *168*, *179*
effort 25

emotions *see* feelings
energy levels, low 5
evolutionary theory 58
expectations, family 47

families
    expectations of 47
    and problem-solving
        85–6
    support from 27–8
family histories, of mental
    health difficulties 54
fear
    responses 7
    of stopping worrying
        127–8
    see also panic attacks
'feeling on edge' 5
'feeling like giving up'
    30–1
feelings (emotions) 38, **39**,
    40, 44, 47
    about worry 38–40,
        39, 44, 47, **56–7**, 61,
        64–5, **66**, 83, 105,
        120, 139
    changes in **39**, **62–3**,
        66, **120**, **191**, **204**
    and struggles with
        emotional wellbeing
        8, 11
friends 28–9, 85–6

general practitioners
    (GPs) 13, 14, 16, 149

generalised anxiety
    disorder (GAD) 3–8, 54
    clinical definition 5–6
    comorbidity with
        depression 8–9
    diagnosis 10
    further resources for
        213–14
    and problem-solving
        53
    severity 6
    symptoms 3–4, 5–6,
        58
    treatment 14
    worry as primary
        feature of 4–5, 58
Generalised Anxiety
    Disorder Questionnaire
    7 (GAD-7) 6, 9–10, *10*,
    21, 34, 70, 119, 127, 157,
    173, **186**
    reviews 30, 142–3,
        166, *168*, **178**, *180*
goal-setting 32, 33–6, 67,
    70, 131, 150, *188–90*
    measurable 34
    and positive framing
        35–6
    realistic 34–5
    and relapse-
        prevention 142, 145
    specific approach to
        33–4
'good' days 27, 34

Harvard Medical School 215
headaches 38
health anxiety 6
hearing 113
hobbies 142
hyper-vigilance 6
hypothetical worries
    definition 49–51
    and recovery stories
        158, 162, 174–5
    and relapse prevention
        135, 140–1
    worry management
        interventions for
        73, *74–7*, 78, 80–2,
        82, 103–4, 109,
        115–16, 118–19,
        121–3

illness anxiety disorder 6
irritability 4, 5

lapses 133–7, 139, 144,
    146, 149
life stresses 2–3, 54, 55
Low Intensity
    Practitioners/Coaches
    13
low mood 8–9, 11, 145

Mandeep (case example)
    19, 20, 40, 49–50
    impact of worry on 61,
        63, 64–5

recovery story 169–78,
    179–80
and relapse prevention
    143, 144, 150–1
and social support
    28–9
story 45–8
and the vicious cycle
    of worry 56, **57**
and worry
    management
    interventions 69,
    73, *76–7*, 107, 110,
    110–11, 117–18
medication 14
mental health difficulties
    58
    family histories of 54
    see also anxiety;
        depression
Mind (charity) 215, 216
mood, low 8–9, 11, 145
muscular tension 4, 6

National Health Service
    (NHS) 13, 16, 59,
    213–15
neurotransmitter
    imbalance 54
NHS Talking Therapies
    for Anxiety and
    Depression services 13,
    16, 214
'NICE guidelines' 14
notOK app 216

'on edge', feeling 5

panic attacks 6–8
    resources for 214–15
    symptoms 7
    thoughts during 7–8
physical (bodily) feelings/
    symptoms 38, **39**, 42,
    46, **56–7**, 61, 65, **66**, 83,
    105, **120**, 139
    changes in 38, **39**, 42,
        46, **62–3**, 65, **66**,
        105, **120**, **191**, **204**
practical worries
    definition 51
    and recovery stories
        159, 162
    and relapse prevention
        140–1
    worry management
        interventions for 73,
        74–7, 78–9, 81–4,
        82, 86–7, 102–3,
        109, 115, 121–3
problem-solving approach
    to worry 27, 52–3, 72,
    81–104, **82**, 109, 115–16
    choosing a solution 94
    identifying solutions
        85–8, *87*, 123–4,
        159–60
    identifying the worry
        84–5, *87*
    impact on the cycle of
        worry 120, **120**

and recovery stories
    161, 174
and relapse-
    prevention 135, 141,
    150
reviewing how it went
    98–102
solution planning
    94–7
solution strengths and
    weakness assessment
    88–94, *89–93*,
    197–200
troubleshooting 122–4
trying the solution 97,
    161
progress reviews 29–30,
    141–3, *206*
psychological, brief
    evidence-based
    treatment 1–2, 59
Psychological Wellbeing
    Practitioners (PWPs)
    13, 16–17, 59

re-focusing attention
    112–14, 124–5, 163, 177
reassurance-seeking 128,
    139
recovery
    stories 22, 41, 153–80
    visualising 33
relapse prevention toolkit
    22, 60–1, 131–51, 168,
    180

constructing your
'toolkit' 137–51
defining lapses 133–7
defining relapses 132,
133–7
and early warning
signs 135, 138–41,
144, 146–7, 149, *168,
179*
and getting further
support 148–9
identifying additional
areas to work on
145–8
identifying practices
that helped improve
things 143–4, *207*
reflecting on how
things have
improved 141–3,
206
top tips 146–8
and the wellbeing
review 144–5
relationships 142
relaxation exercises 4, 215
restlessness 3, 4, 5

sadness 38
self-beliefs
of being unable to
manage difficulties 4
positive self-beliefs
about worry 52–3,
54

that worry will result
in harm 38
self-compassion 30
self-criticism 147
self-harm 11–12, 46–7,
171, 216
distraction techniques
for 47
self-help 15–16
see also CBT self-help
senses 113–14
setbacks 27, 138
see also relapse
prevention toolkit
sight 113
single-parents *see* Therese
(case example)
sleep problems 4, 6, 38,
42, 46, 139
smell, sense of 113
social anxiety 6
social lives 142
Stay Alive app 126
stress 2–3
as cause of worry 54,
55
short-term 5
stress response,
exaggerated 7
students *see* Mandeep
suicidal thoughts 11, 216
transitory nature 11
support 27–8, 30–3
getting further help
148–9

taste, sense of 114
Therese (case example)
19, 20, 40, 49
impact of worry on 61,
62, 64–5
recovery story 153–66,
167–8
and relapse prevention
140–1, 143, 144,
150–1
and social support
28–9
story 41–4
and the vicious cycle
of worry 56, **56**
and worry
management
interventions 69, 73,
74–5, 85, 94–6, 98–9
thoughts
cascades of 55
changes in **39**, 41–3,
45–7, **62–3**, 65, **66**,
105, **120**, **191**, **204**
'what if...?' thinking
37, 49, 53, 55, **56–7**,
62–3, *74–7*, *110–11*,
158
worries as 49–52
and worry 38–9, **39**,
41–3, 45–7, **56–7**,
61, 64, **66**, 83, 105,
120, 139
threat perception 58
tiredness/fatigue 3, 5

touch, sense of 113
treatment options 12–17
cognitive behavioural
therapy 14–15
medication 14
professional support
12–13
self-help 15–16
see also CBT self-
help; relapse
prevention toolkit;
worry management
interventions
triggers for worry 55,
140–1
troubleshooting 24, 28,
121–9

uncertainty 43, 53, 128

vicious cycle of worry 52,
55–6, **56–7**, 65–7, 70–1,
131, 136, 173
virtuous cycles 65–7, **66**,
71
visualising recovery 33

wellbeing, emotional 8, 11
wellbeing reviews 144–5,
147, *167–8*, *179–80*,
208–9
wellbeing teams 148
'what if...?' thinking 37,
49, 53, 55, **56–7**, **62–3**,
74–7, *110–11*, 158

work-related worries
41–2, *87*, *89–93*, 142,
166–7
workbook 9, 18, 22–3, 26,
31–2, 181–212
  graph for plotting
    GAD-7 score
    progress **166**, **178**,
    186
  notes 181–4
  Worksheet 1 (Weekly
    record of GAD-7
    score) 9, 70, 143, *185*
  Worksheet 2 (Making
    change happen) 31,
    187
  Worksheet 3 (My
    goals) 35–6, 70, 142,
    188–90
  Worksheet 4 (How is
    worry affecting you?)
    64–5, 70, 139, **191**
  Worksheet 5 (Worry
    diary) 73, *74–7*, 78,
    81–2, 84, 104, 144,
    158, 162, 163, 173–5,
    192–3
  Worksheet 6
    (Problem-solving)
    83, 84, *87*, 88, 94, 97,
    100, 116, 135, *194–6*
  Worksheet 7
    (Strengths and
    weaknesses) 88–9,
    89–93, 93, *197–200*

Worksheet 8 (Worry
  time list) 107, 112,
  115, 201, *201–2*
Worksheet 9 (Worry
  time review) 116,
  203
Worksheet 10 (My
  early warning signs)
  138–9, **204**
Worksheet 11 (My
  most significant
  early warning signs)
  139, *205*
Worksheet 12 (Positive
  improvements
  achieved over
  treatment) 141–2,
  206
Worksheet 13
  (Things that
  helped me achieve
  improvements) 143,
  168, *180*, *207*
Worksheet 14
  (Wellbeing reviews)
  144, *208–9*
Worksheet 15 (Issues
  to work on in the
  future) 145, *210–11*
Worksheet 16 (Useful
  sources of support)
  149, *212*
World Health
Organization (WHO)
213

worry 1–36
  and behaviour 38,
    38–9, 39, **39**, 41–3,
    46–7, **56–7**, 61, 64,
    66, 83, 105, **120**,
    128, 139
  being unable to stop
    38
  belief it will result in
    harm 38
  causes of 54–7, **56–7**
  classification 72–82,
    74–7, **82**, 84–5,
    121–3, 173–4
  definition 2–3, 49
  disproportionate 3, 52
  early warning signs of
    60, 135, 138–41, 144,
    146–7, 149, *168*, *179*
  evolutionary theory
    of 58
  excessive 3
  and external factors 21
  fear of stopping
    worrying 127–8
  features of 38–40, **39**,
    41
  and feelings 38–40,
    39, 44, 47, **56–7**, 61,
    64–5, **66**, 83, 105,
    120, 139
  function 40–8, 58
  hypothetical worries
    49–51, 73, *74–7*, 78,
    80–2, **82**, 103–4,

    109, 115–16, 118–19,
    121–3, 135, 140–1,
    158, 162, 174–5
  impact 61–7, **62–3**, **66**
  lack of control over 41
  'letting go of' 104–5,
    125
  as life-limiting
    experience 32
  long-term tendency
    to 5
  persistent 3, 38, 40–8,
    51–2, 57–8
  physical symptoms 38,
    39, 42, 46
  positive beliefs about
    52–3, 54
  practical worries 51,
    73, *74–7*, 78–9,
    81–4, **82**, 86–7,
    102–3, 109, 115,
    121–3, 140–1, 159,
    162
  as a process 53–4
  psychological, brief
    evidence-based
    treatment 1–2,
    59
  recovery stories 22, 41,
    153–80
  recurrent 60–1
  relapse prevention
    toolkit 22, 60–1,
    131–51
  sufferers 57–8

and thoughts 38–9, **39**, 41–3, 45–7, **56–7**, 61, **62–3**, 64–5, **66**, 83, 105, **120**, 139, **191**, **204**
treatment options 12–17
triggers 55, 140–1
understanding 21, 36, 37–67
urgent worries 109
vicious cycle of 52, 55–6, **56–7**, 65–7, 70–1, 131, 136, 173
visualising recovery 33
what can be done to stop 59
why do worries escalate? 52–4
workbook 9, 18, 22–3, 26, 31–2, 181–212
worry management interventions 21–2, 44, 69–129, 131
definition 72
and relapse-prevention 140–1, 147–8
troubleshooting 121–9
worry classification 72–82, *74–7*, **82**, 84–5, 121–3, 173–4
worry management 72, 81, **82**, 104–20, **120**, 164–5, 175–7

see also problem-solving approach to worry; recovery stories; relapse prevention toolkit; worry time
worry postponement technique 114
worry time 81, **82**, 104–20, **120**, 164–5, 175–7
feeling uncomfortable during 125–6
and re-focusing your attention 112–14, 124–5, 163, 177
and relapse-prevention 135
scheduling 105, 106–7, 108
and troubleshooting 124–7
using 115–20
when to stop 126–7
Worksheet 8 (Worry time list) 107, 112, 115, 201, *201–2*
worry time review 116, 116–18, *203*
and writing worries down 108–12, *110–11*
worst-case scenarios 43, 53, **56**, 86, 136
writing things down 108–12, *110–11*, 150–1